Catharine Merrill

**The Soldier of Indiana in the War for the Union**

Catharine Merrill

**The Soldier of Indiana in the War for the Union**

ISBN/EAN: 9783337309183

Printed in Europe, USA, Canada, Australia, Japan

Cover: Foto ©ninafisch / pixelio.de

More available books at **www.hansebooks.com**

THE

# SOLDIER OF INDIANA

IN THE

## WAR FOR THE UNION.

"Let all the ends thou aimst at be thy country's,
Thy God's, and truth's."— SHAKSPEARE.

INDIANAPOLIS:
MERRILL AND COMPANY.
1864.

WHO HAVE GIVEN MORE TO THEIR COUNTRY THAN THE

Mothers, Wives, and Sisters

OF THE

SOLDIERS OF INDIANA?

TO THEM IS THIS RECORD OF THE HEROISM OF
SON, HUSBAND, BROTHER,

*DEDICATED.*

# PREFACE.

On July 10th, 1862, we issued a circular, which was mailed to the officers of every Indiana regiment, soliciting such information as would enable us to prepare a complete record of the part taken by our State in the suppression of the Rebellion. In addition to a full narration, we proposed to give the names of all Indianians who had fallen in their country's service, if not of all who had enrolled themselves in her armies. We expected to commence the issue of our work as early as September, 1862.

Circumstances, however, delayed publication until the present time, and also compelled a modification of our plan, especially in regard to the catalogue of names. The men of Indiana must blame their own patriotism, so promptly, largely, and gloriously displayed that it would require the compass of an encyclopædia to contain individual names.

In the prosecution of our work, we have had serious difficulties to encounter. Sometimes it has been next to impossible to decide between contradictory, or to reconcile incongruous statements. Sometimes we have been unable to obtain particulars of some interesting event. And sometimes, again, while we have had full and clear accounts of the part one regiment has taken in an action, we have had very slight information in regard to the equally important part borne in the same action by another.

These difficulties continue, and perhaps will continue throughout our work.

While we cannot deprecate all criticism without throwing aside all claim to merit, we yet, in view of the difficulties and obstacles with which we have had to contend, and in view of our earnest and honest desire to do justice to patriot and traitor, ask the indulgence of soldier and civilian.

We owe our thanks to the many who have aided us with information: to the soldiers who have allowed their letters to be at our service; to the editor of the "Indianapolis Daily Journal," for files of that paper; to Mrs. Judge Orth, for the use of her valuable scrap-books; to Mr. Davies, of Rensselaer; to Lieutenant E. E. Bassett, some of whose pages, though not prepared for publication, we have embodied in the sketch of the Bracken Rangers; and to Dr. Fletcher, whose private papers, written for the information and entertainment of his own family, we have freely used, a little perhaps to his surprise, but we trust to the gratification of the public. Others, too numerous to mention, have given us valuable assistance.

With these words we give to the public this venture. Though it might seem immodest, perhaps ungenerous, to claim that our State, whose sons have fought beside the sons of all her loyal sisters, encircling the Rebellion with her regiments, is *prima*, yet we may be allowed to say, that, wherever any of the sisterhood, emulous in valor, endurance, and devotion to the Union of the States, have made themselves conspicuous, there has proudly stood Indiana *inter pares*.

Let those surpass her in the generous strife who can.

MERRILL & CO.

*April*, 1864.

# THE SOLDIER OF INDIANA

IN THE

## WAR FOR THE UNION.

### CHAPTER I.

#### INTRODUCTION.

INDIANA is a young State with forests yet uncut, with swamps undrained, and fertile accessible soil untouched by the plough; but she encloses within her borders, and shelters under her laws, a population of near a million and a half, — representatives of every country in Europe. The history of Vincennes and Fort Wayne dates back to the time of Louis le Grand, when missionaries and traders led small colonies, and ambitious statesmen sent military forces across the ocean and along the lakes to isolated western wildernesses for the promotion of their several objects; and to this day the customs and language of the French of that period may be found to some extent in the region of these towns. Swiss have cultivated the sunny slopes of the Ohio since the beginning of the present century. Irish in great numbers have within the last twenty years established themselves along the railroads and in centres of business. Germans, their thrifty hands having gathered silver in city employments, possess and cultivate farms in every county. English and Scotch give their national peculiarities to many a small settlement. Norwegians and Laplanders sprinkle the northern districts. In addition to these members of the Caucasian race numbers of negroes live independently and somewhat lazily along Blue River and in other comfortable regions, and a few Indians fish, hunt, and do some small trading where through sufferance they remain.

Beholding this motley population, the transatlantic stranger, and even the friendly countryman from the western shores of the unfriendly ocean, are ready to declare that Indiana can have no oneness, and in consequence no distinctive character; that, with materials unfitted and unfitting if not mutually abhorrent, she is and must long remain an unconglomerate mass. The inference is incorrect. A large majority of the population is of one stock,—the sturdy old English,—which, under the stirring influences of the seventeenth century, spread along the Atlantic coast from the bleak rocks of Maine to near tropical regions. Through the vicissitudes of time and repeated emigration, the characteristics of the English of that period have been retained. Indomitable energy, ineradicable love of home, unquenchable and deep-buried enthusiasm, only called forth by stroke of steel, and "that spirit of personal independence which may be sharpened into insolence or educated into manly self-respect," are as remarkable in the feller of Indiana forests, and the ploughman of Indiana prairies, as they were in the self-exiled Puritan or Cavalier;—and they form the outline of Indiana as they do of all American character.

The filling up of this fine hard English outline is the material derived from the various sources alluded to, and modified by as great a variety of circumstances. It is neither mean nor common, nor is it Irish, nor German, nor Swiss, nor Yankee, nor Southern. Like a grand piece of mosaic in which all colors are united to the obscuring of none, and the enhancing of the lustre of each, the typical Hoosier is dependent on every element for completeness, yet as a whole is dissimilar to any part. He is sensitive, excitable, bashful, and it may be boastful, enterprising, ardent, and industrious; yet, as a farmer, is apt to leave weeds in his fence corners, and as a merchant dislikes to bother his brains with one cent calculations. He is no bully, yet is able to use his fist, and if he is accused of lying,—the vice most repugnant to his nature,— he loses not a moment in applying his fist in a free fight. In early times when an application to law required long and inconvenient journeys, he administered justice in a somewhat summary method: giving notice to an individual who disturbed a neighborhood to remove, and if the notice was disregarded, administering a hickory limb or displacing a cabin roof. No other approach to mob-law has the genuine Indianian ever known; even in the case of an obnoxious neighbor his first impulse invariably was to join the weaker party; and he gave it up only when satisfied that neither justice nor generosity required its defence.

A decidedly religious stamp was given to Indiana character by the preachers of an early day, — often men of intellect as well as zeal, who found their way to the backwoods and preached Christ from a cabin-door, or from the shade of a spreading beech, to the sunburnt men and women gathered from the region round about. Many an old man now recalls with a thrill the majestic or fiery eloquence of an Armstrong, a Ray, or a Strange, as it rang through the Gothic aisles of the primeval forest. To those fervid laborers was it owing that the little church was erected as soon as the log-cabin afforded the shelter of a home. The contemptuous application of "North C'lina Church" to men of notoriously worldly or otherwise wicked character, implies a classification of a community which is significant of religious character.

Many of the early lawyers were men of rare wit and literary attainments, but they did not, like their preaching contemporaries, permanently influence the character of society.

Indiana's resources for material wealth are vast, and being rapidly developed. Little distinction in the condition of citizens exists. A man might perhaps number the rich on his fingers, and certainly could the beggars, except such as the Old World has sent over the ocean with cards certifying to an escape from a shipwreck or a volcano.

No young State shows finer institutions of learning or of charity. Yet many a boy never sees the inside of a schoolhouse, and many a man drops into the ballot-box a vote he cannot read, and makes the cross instead of his name to a deed of sale or purchase.

There are in every community men who seem to be Nature's step-sons, rather than the sons of the bond-woman,

— their hand against every man, and themselves the object of every man's upraised hand or foot. They form that floating population which is invariably borne on the first wave of the tide of civilization, and is the deadly foe to the true precursors of progress, — the farmer, the peddler, and the preacher. They form, too, that deposit which lies normally at the base, but penetrates sometimes to the very top of the mass of society. They are the fighting, hating, bitter, grasping element, — aristocrats in one position, levellers in another. The objects of their special hate in our western world are three: the negro, the abolitionist, and, somewhat inconsistently, the aristocrat.

The first murder in the capital of our State was committed by a member of a small but notorious association called the Chain-gang, formed for the purpose of spattering the three objects of detestation with rotten eggs; of giving them nocturnal airings astride of rails, and of indulging in other disorderly and lawless proceedings. The sight of a son of a Philadelphia clergyman, — a young school-teacher who wore kid gloves and fashionable pantaloons, in those days called "tights," — inflamed the wrath of one of the Chain-gang to such a degree that nothing but death could appease its intensity. He was ferryman, and one fair day pushed from the shore of White River with the unsuspicious young gentleman in his boat. In mid-stream the offence was expiated. The ferryman reached the farther shore alone. For this most cruel deed the perpetrator suffered an imprisonment of two years in the penitentiary. That pardon is more effectual than chastisement in the correction of crime, seems to be a principle of Indiana officials, as such leniency is by no means uncommon.

The last victim of these murderous rowdies was a negro, who, on the Fourth of July, had the impudence to walk on the pavement of Washington Street.

The links of the Chain-gang have long lain in the dust, or rusted in the wilderness beyond the Mississippi; but passions do not die; and in the far more pretentious and widely extended Golden Circle we find a new embodiment of the principle of the ancient Chain-gang.

At the first election for Governor in 1816, on the admission of the Territory of Indiana into the Union as a State, the contest naturally turned on the question of slavery. Settlers from free and slave States were about equal in number, but the friends from North Carolina voted with the emigrants from the eastern and middle States, and the anti-slavery candidate was elected. As the question was entirely local, party lines of distinction rising from slavery were soon effaced, and slavery was for many years a subject of neither political nor social interest. A certain soreness, however, was produced, and kept alive, by the escape of a slave, at rare intervals, in or through Indiana.

In 1824 or 1825, an individual informed a handsome slave-woman, Nellie, who was accompanying her master from Virginia to Missouri, that Indiana was free soil. In consequence she refused to proceed on the journey, and the master had resort to law. Judge Morris of Indianapolis, before whom the case was tried, pronounced the woman free. Judge Park of the Supreme Court, to which the exasperated master appealed, reversed the decision. Meantime the woman had fled, and she could not for several weeks be found. At last she was traced to a cabin occupied by a widow, on the bluffs of White River. The sheriff with his attendants appeared unexpectedly at the door. Admittance was delayed, and while they waited, the woman of the house, her head enveloped in Nellie's bright colored handkerchief, sprang from the back window, and ran like a deer towards the woods. With a whoop and hurrah, like hunters when the game is in sight, the servants of the law followed. The moment they turned, the cabin-door opened, and with stealthy steps the fugitive, guided by a young girl, the daughter of the kind countrywoman, sought and found shelter in a neighboring cave. But Nellie was betrayed. With twenty dollars the sheriff beguiled the girl to point out her hiding-place. Incidents of this kind, serving as they did to awaken sympathies which otherwise would have lain dormant, were like drops gathering for the long delayed storm.

From the time of General Jackson's election to the Presidency in 1828, party spirit became warm in Indiana as everywhere else, although it was not until 1840 that national politics exercised a controlling influence in the election of State officers. During the following twelve years party spirit ran with great violence; but the defeat sustained by the Whig party, not only in Indiana but throughout the Union, in 1852, terminated its existence. In 1854, the slumbering volcano, which had shaken the nation in 1820, and again in 1850, was a third time evoked by a repeal of the Missouri Compromise.

The fathers of the Republic, with the fact that slavery had been forced upon them by the mother-country in spite of clerical and legislative opposition fresh in their minds, and incapable of imagining their descendants seduced into an affection for and an approval of so vast an evil, regarded it as doomed to gradual extinction. The middle of the nineteenth century found many willing defenders of what they called a divine institution. The citizens of the free States, opposed in principle and feeling to slavery, regarded it as the charge if not the curse of the South, and as such were unwilling to trouble themselves with it; and yielded again and again to its repeated claims for protection. Many young politicians, blinded by personal ambition, gave their voices to the support of Southern views for the sake of obtaining Southern votes. In 1820 the State of Missouri was given up to slavery, freedom receiving from slavery in return the territory north of 36° 30′. In 1854 slavery denounced the existence of this barrier as a reproach and stigma, and insisted that the territory of Kansas which lay above the slave line, and was calling for admission into the sisterhood of States, should be received as a slave State.

Opposition to this demand united large numbers of Democrats and Whigs with the small party of Free-soilers, and formed a new organization styling itself the Republican party, which by force of circumstances was confined almost exclusively to the free States. A small party ignoring the slavery question was organized, and called itself the Know-nothing or American party. The old Democratic name was kept by those who were in favor of letting the people of each Terri- tory determine what should be the character of its institutions as a State. This party carried the election of 1856 Indiana voting with it.

Emigrants poured into Kansas from the North, determined that it should be a free State; from the South, determined that it should be a slave State. Civil war, with horrors and outrages unparelleled, resulted. Prominent in this strife on the anti-slavery side was an old man, who, two years later, was to shake the nation from centre to circumference. This man, hating slavery as a personal enemy which had murdered his sons, as well as an enemy to human rights, conceived it his mission to destroy the monster. With an adaptation of means to the end proposed, worthy of insanity, he took twenty-two men, five of them of the oppressed race, organized in Canada a provisional government of the United States, with himself as Commander-in-chief, and penetrated to the mountains of Virginia, whither he had arms secretly shipped to furnish those who should join him.

Sunday night, October 16, 1859, he seized the unsuspecting village of Harper's Ferry and took possession of the United States Armory. The nation was astonished, electrified, at the boldness of the attempt. State and national troops poured to the spot, but were held at bay by the old man for thirty hours, when, having lost two sons and eleven others of his twenty-two, and having been himself repeatedly and seriously wounded, he was overpowered. The fanaticism, as it was almost universally called, North as well as South, of John Brown, was equalled by the unflinching bravery, sturdy independence, patient endurance, and grim, puritanic piety which extorted the admiration even of those who demanded and took his life as the expiation of his crime. These traits were remarkably exemplified when the magnanimous mother of Presidents carried to her bar on his couch her wounded, helpless prisoner, — pushed on his trial with unseemly haste to conviction and the death sentence, and guarded the short remnant of the life allowed him, — which common humanity would have deemed properly passed in a secure hospital, — by thousands of her soldiers from the danger of an imaginary rescue to the scaffold.

This was in December 1859. In less than eighteen months

regiments of United States troops marched through the streets of the most conservative city of the North singing to a wild simple melody —

"John Brown's body lies a-mouldering in the grave,
But his soul is marching on!"

The growth in the North of the sentiment of opposition to the extension of slavery, together with the division of the Democratic party, brought about by those who have since led in the attempt to divide the Union, insured the election of a Republican President in 1860; Lincoln being elected by a plurality 30,000 larger than elected his predecessor. The vote of Indiana, one of the most conservative States, had changed from a Republican minority of 46,681 to a majority of 5,923.

Although a Republican President was constitutionally elected, the judicial and legislative branches of the government were in the opposition, and would have remained so through his term of office, so that no offensive measures could have been passed, nor even objectionable cabinet ministers appointed. Not only this, Congress declared its willingness to incorporate into the Constitution a clause utterly prohibiting interference with slavery in the States.

The loyal States, together with those which were trembling in the balance, sent delegates to a pacificatory convention presided over by an Ex-President of the United States, who as President having betrayed the party which elected him, has since eclipsed his old disgrace by the crime of treason to his country. Among Indiana's delegates to this convention were Mr. Lincoln's Secretary of the Interior and General Hackleman, who lately gave his life to his country on the field of Shiloh.

But no honorable concessions could satisfy those who had predetermined the destruction of the Government. They understood better than the North itself the deep significance of the election of Lincoln. It was an assurance to them that a spirit had moved upon the face of the chaos into which the political parties of the North had crumbled, and that they must break or be broken upon the new creation. It was an assurance that the power, which had not only filled the presidential chair and courts of law, term after term, but had underreached and overreached, had misconstrued and misapplied the Constitution, until the simplicity and integrity of that document seemed forever gone, had reached its flood. And it was an assurance, — but even the far-reaching statesmen of the South did not recognize this, — of the upheaving of the heads of the everlasting rocks of justice, and of the utterance of the long silent divine voice: " No farther, ye waves of barbarism, shall ye go!"

The politicians of the South had not waited for this hour. More than thirty years every art known to them, — and no politicians are so wily as those of a Republic, — had been used to bring the Southern public into subjection to an oligarchy. Society itself from its very base passively seconded their efforts. The upper, middle, and lower classes which are usually found in civilized nations, and which the most democratic communities have never yet been able to abrogate, are here merged into two, standing at a formidable and almost impassable distance. The common saying that " poor people are mean," harsh as may be the sentiment, is not incorrect in the society in which it originated. The poor whites of the South are monstrously degraded. Red-skinned savages were never more malicious and bloodthirsty. In the older slave States they are lazier and feebler than the corresponding class in the North: they submit without resistance to kicks, cuffs, and blows; but let them scent the negro or the abolitionist and they are no longer listless and spiritless: their sallow visages light up, their skinny fingers clutch the rifle or the stone, and they are as keen as bloodhounds. Yet wide as the barrier between them, the proud and selfish slaveholders, whose souls swelled with the endeavor to grasp the aggrandizement a future, independent of the plodding North, seemed to offer, and the luckless, slaveless dwellers of sandy or marshy regions, whose only foothold for pride is the inferior position of the negro, have one common ancestry, — for whether descended from convict or cavalier, their origin is English; as the harsh, coarse hate which distinguishes both, if not peculiar to the Anglo-Saxon, is at least incontestably one of his characteristics, until eradicated by intellectual refinement or religious principle; and is so certainly alien to the French that it can be no heirloom of the noble Huguenots who sought a refuge on the west Atlantic coast, and who, excepting a few Spaniards, were the only other white settlers. They had also one common ground of interest and affection, and they burned with one common desire " to carry war to the densely populated cities of the North, which offered food for the sword and the torch, and to make the grass grow on the pavements now worn off by commerce."* The stream of emigration which set in from European shores early in the present century, carried a large proportion, especially within later years, of Irish emigrants to the South, where the element of disorder, inherent in the son of Erin, readily assimilated with the revolutionary tendencies of slavery — aristocracy and objectless discontent.

Immediately after the election of Lincoln, South Carolina with dramatic dignity announced her determination to secede from the Union. Secession was assumed to be a Constitutional right, and the provocation sufficient to warrant the assertion of that right. The North was incredulous and amused. Amusement became derision; derision intensified itself to scorn, and scorn blazed into a vast indignation when the little arrogant sovereignty officially and formally carried her announcement into effect; and one by one nearly every other slave State followed her leading.

* Speech of Jeff. Davis in Stevenson, Alabama, February, 1861.

## CHAPTER II.

### THE UPRISING.

APRIL 12, 1861, the telegraph flashed through the Union the intelligence that a United States fort on the coast of South Carolina — Fort Sumter — was bombarded. No man living within the limits of America will ever forget that despatch. The old earth itself seemed to reel under a blow, and no longer to afford a sure foothold. Through the long Saturday that followed, business was at a stand; business houses were closed, and men with clinched fists and high-beating hearts stood on the street-corners and at the doors of the telegraph office. That night, from the knobs of the Ohio to the sand-hills of Lake Michigan, from the Quaker towns on the eastern border to the prairie farms on the western line, the streets of Indiana were black with breathless multitudes still awaiting tidings of the seventy loyal men in an unfinished fort, bombarded by ten thousand raging rebels! When the banner appeared, — the banner which within the memory of the present generation had only idly fluttered in holiday breezes, — a new meaning seemed to stream from its folds: hats were taken off as in the presence of something sacred; and shouts, beginning, it might be, brokenly and in tears, rose and swelled and made walls and skies resound.

At ten o'clock a despatch was announced: "Sumter has fallen." Young men and men in middle life looked at the white faces and wet eyes of old and venerated citizens who stood in the street waiting for tidings, and a great stillness fell upon all. They turned to separate and creep silently to their homes. Another despatch! "Mr. Lincoln will issue a Proclamation to-morrow, calling for seventy-five thousand volunteers." Cheer upon cheer, roar upon roar responded. The white-faced old men grew red: they stamped, pounded, wept, roared with the loudest, wildest, and maddest. Good, cold-blooded people who had gone to bed, sprang up, threw open their windows, screamed to passers-by for information, and joined, too, in the national shout.

Sunday the tidings and events of the preceding day and night seemed like an insane dream; and the crowd again hung about the doors of telegraph and newspaper offices, but with anxious sickening hearts they turned away, when the night's intelligence was confirmed past the shadow of a doubt, and laid their grief and dread at the foot of the God of Nations. The voice of congregation and choir this day reunited in the utterance of national songs, and sanctified them.

Governor Morton's proclamation followed the President's. Indiana's quota of the seventy-five thousand was six thousand. Governor Morton's proclamation was the blast of a war-trumpet. The clerk dropped his pen, the woodman his axe, the ploughman left his plough in the furrow, the machinist his hammer beside the locomotive boiler; and before the blast had died away in the forest and over the waves of Lake Michigan, fifteen thousand stalwart soldiers stood ready for war. Gray-haired men who had thought themselves prepared to depart in peace prayed that they might be longer spared. Not content with prayers, many a shaking hand took down the rusted rifle.

"No, no. You have served your country long enough," replied a captain to an applicant who had fought in the battle of the Thames. By dint of colored hair and beard, one old soldier of the war of 1812 found his way into the ranks, and was mustered in with men young enough to be his grandsons. "If I were only four years younger!" sighed Major Whitlock, the contemporary of General Harrison. "Ninety is not too old in such a cause; and the young people know nothing of war. Fifty years of profound peace have made no soldiers."

Men who had more money than muscle did not lag behind in generosity. Winslow and Lanier of New York, the latter formerly an Indiana man, offered Governor Morton twenty-five thousand dollars. William Morrison of Indianapolis, one thousand. T. J. Brooks of Loogootee, to Captain Kimball's company, one thousand dollars. The Indianapolis Branch of the Bank of the State, donated one thousand dollars for the use of Marion County volunteers and their families. Evansville gave fifteen thousand dollars. Madison, six thousand dollars. The little towns gave without stint to the families of volunteers. Union City, with a population of less than one thousand, and not a rich man in the number, gave fourteen hundred dollars. Noblesville, twenty-five thousand dollars, collected at an evening meeting, within a few minutes. Cass County, six thousand dollars; Elkhart County, eight thousand dollars; Greensburg, two thousand dollars; Winchester, almost one thousand. The limits of a Gazetteer, alone, would suffice for a full enumeration. Farmers, without the slightest thought or desire for remuneration, bestowed their best horses; women robbed their chests of well-preserved blankets, and, dropping household needlework, sewed day and night on soldiers' shirts and drawers.

The legislature, which met in pursuance of a call from Governor Morton, April 24, transacted business without the utterance of a party-word. The officers in both Senate and House were elected unanimously; — perhaps the State-House of Indiana will never again present such a spectacle.

In agreement with a suggestion in the Message of Governor Morton, arrangements were made for the disposal of surplus troops, and an appropriation of one million dollars for army purposes.

The volunteers, almost without exception, made pecuniary sacrifices: leaving positions on railroads and farms, in shops and offices, all of which were respectable, and if not lucrative, were at least comfortable. They rose in haste at their country's call, with no time nor heart to count the cost, but ready to give all. Would the means be forthcoming? Would the way to action be opened? In the words of the adjutant-general: "The citizens of Indiana, belonging almost exclusively to the agricultural class, had been devotedly engaged, — since the earliest settlement of the State, beginning with the close of the war of 1812, — in the peaceful pursuit of clearing away the forests, cutting roads, and in various ways developing the vast resources of her fertile soil. Thus for nearly fifty years peace had held her willing sway, until the conviction had almost escaped the minds of men that every able-bodied man in the nation was bound to do his country military service in times of threatened public danger. Probably at no period in the world's history has a people been found so little prepared for war."

The military institutions of Indiana consisted of a quartermaster-general and an adjutant-general, — who filled the offices for some such sum as one hundred dollars annually, — and of a militia which existed only in name.

The preceding winter Hon. Lewis Wallace, now General Wallace, drew up a bill modelled after the law of Massachusetts, and labored earnestly to have it pass the legislature for the organization of State militia. It failed, and when the outbreak came there were, perhaps, five independent companies in existence. There was not a shotted cartridge in the State; not enough effective arms for a single regiment; no knapsacks, haversacks, canteens, — in short, a total lack of camp and garrison equipage. The States are each entitled to a certain allowance of arms; but Indiana had made no requisition on the Government, and in consequence had not for several years received any arms.

The finances of Indiana were in a lower condition than they had been for twenty years. The State treasury was empty. The school-fund had been largely drawn upon to defray the expenses of the Government, including the pay of the legislature. Moreover the new governor had not been elected to the office. It had fallen upon him because his superior had accepted a place in the United States Senate. His executive abilities were unknown. Under these circumstances, it was a hundred-fold more difficult to raise means for the subsistence, equipment, and transportation of six thousand troops, than it would have been to form an army of twenty thousand men. But if any man in the United States has a right to look the nation in the face and say, "I have done my duty," that man is Governor Morton.

The day before the President's Proclamation was issued he sent two agents to the eastern cities and one to Canada, to make arrangements for procuring arms and equipments. Immediately after the Proclamation he summoned Lewis

Wallace, Esq., of Crawfordsville, to assume the office of adjutant-general. Before the 27th of April the six required regiments were organized and formed into a brigade, with Thomas A. Morris, brigadier-general; John Love, brigade inspector with the rank of major; and Milo S. Hascall, aide-de-camp, with the rank of captain. These gentlemen were all educated at West Point, and possessed of experience and ability. They assembled the throngs of volunteers, who were streaming to the capital from every part of the State, in a beautiful grove north of the city, where for many years Methodist camp-meetings had been held; established a military camp, and named the formerly sacred spot, in honor of the governor, Camp Morton.

The regiments were numbered not from one, but from six, out of respect, it was publicly said, for the five regiments engaged in the Mexican war, and for the purpose of preventing historical confusion. It was privately suggested, that the cause lay deeper in the unenviable reputation gained by the Indiana Second in the Mexican war, — a reputation now understood to have been undeservedly bestowed by Jeff Davis, in the selfish desire to exonerate himself and his Mississippians. But not even a slandered number should be affixed to an Indiana regiment. Not the stern Roman of unrivalled renown was more jealous of his honor, than the young State which had yet no history.

The subordinate officers knew little or nothing of military rules or discipline, but they made up in diligence for what was lacking in intelligence. Men who had scarcely opened a book since freed from the trammels of school, became violent devotees to learning. Hardee's "Tactics" came suddenly into requisition; dictionaries, English and French, were equally in demand. Pupils and teachers alternated; and every secluded spot in the neighborhood of Camp Morton was converted either into a class-room or a private study. Privates were often not more ignorant than their officers; yet being more numerous were the butt of many a good-natured jest, especially the strapping farmer youths who were following the plough in their bare feet when the war summons came, and joined the ranks unshod. It was said, that the technical terms "right and left" were entirely above their comprehension, and that it was necessary to substitute the familiar words "gee and haw."

Between the words traitor and poison there seems to be a relationship, at least one is suggestive of the other; and as it was known that traitors existed even in Indianapolis, — although now the boldest traitor dared not utter a word in the face of the tempest of public opinion, — rumors of poisoning soon excited attention and suspicion. The power of imagination was never better illustrated than by the sudden convulsions into which some in camp were thrown, in consequence of eating oranges and drinking water reported to be poisoned; and by the instantaneous cure effected by the sight of the young post-surgeon coolly and with impunity partaking of the poisoned fruit and water. Men were actually cast into and snatched from the very gripe of death.

There was, however, genuine sickness in camp. The rough impromptu hospital was soon filled, and one stormy midnight a man died. Poor soul; he had done nothing for the cause which had stirred his enthusiasm, but then he had had no long marches, no hungry days, no weary, sleepless nights, no neglect and abuse as hundreds and thousands of others have had who since have died like him seemingly to no purpose!

The President's Proclamation, which stirred Indiana and all the North to their very depths, was to the unruly spirits of Virginia and Maryland, which together encircle the District of Columbia, what the spark is to the well-laid train of gunpowder. Without awaiting the action of convention or legislature they threatened the capital, and made it necessary to order troops to Washington immediately after an army had been called into existence. In obedience to the summons a regiment of Massachusetts soldiers arrived at Baltimore, on the way to the capital, — April 19, as it happened, — the anniversary of the day on which the first blow for independence was struck in 1775. A mob, excited to madness by individuals who themselves remained quiet and undiscovered, attacked the soldiers before they had left the train and while they were still unarmed, and shed there, — in the streets of a city of Maryland, Massachusetts blood. Sacred blood! The first to be poured out in the assertion of independence,— the first in defence of the Constitution!

Five weeks later a whisper thrilled all the North,— a whisper (for no man dared say aloud) that a Rebel hand had fired into the heart of Ellsworth. Ellsworth was a poor, laborious young student, and small was the circle of his acquaintance; but with his uplifted hand tearing down, his eager foot trampling on, the emblem of the traitor, his impulsive heart pierced and bleeding, he stood to the nation a type of the greatness and the woe which now hung over her youth.

## CHAPTER III.

### WEST VIRGINIA.

VIRGINIA was dragged out of the Union. Her people were opposed to Secession. When the Convention, elected by a large Union majority to discuss the subject, passed the Ordinance of Secession, the State presented, what was now no longer an anomaly, the spectacle of the executive officers of the Government, elected by the people, on one side, and the people themselves on the other. Emissaries, however, with arguments as various as the minds which form a community,— a pistol ostentatiously worn,— a Minie ball, with a hole perforated, tied to a button,— a promise of position or a specious misrepresentation,— achieved unanimity of opinion in East Virginia and in the Valley. But west of the Alleghanies lay a district which defied treason, however it might be enforced, or in whatever guise it might be arrayed. This region, in its alienation from the older parts of the State, affords not the least among the many striking proofs of the preservation or restoration of mediæval traits in the slave States. In Europe, in those times when communication between lands separated by mountains was so difficult as to be almost impossible, nations lay side by side in entire ignorance — or in ignorance enlightened only by travelling monks — each of the laws, customs, and language of the other; even the same nation, divided by the emigration of a colony, or a roving tribe, beyond a mountain-chain, grew in its parts unlike and often inimical. It might be imagined that, in our new country, time had not sufficed to alienate any one portion of the population, especially of the same State, from any other portion. But with the assistance of numerous secondary agents, not much time is necessary to rust the strongest bonds of union.

Poor sons of Virginia climbed the Alleghanies, settled on the Cheat, the Kanawha, and the Big Sandy, and grew to be another people. In the course of time, it is true, two fine roads were made across the mountains: the northern, over the triple ranges of Laurel Hill, Cheat, and Alleghany, from Parkersburg on the Ohio, through Clarksburg, Philippi, Buckhannon, and Beverly, to Staunton, in the Valley; the southern, from Charleston across the Gauley to Lewisburg; but the journey along these roads was long and laborious, and never could be undertaken unless prompted by necessity or the demands of the warmest affection. No railroad to this day disturbs the old-time quiet which prevails in all but the northern line of West Virginia. There was little then of intercourse to keep alive old affections, or to preserve old ties of any character.

Much, on the contrary, tended to dissimilarity in character and estrangement in feeling. Scarcity of slaves obliged the new settlers to regard free labor with favor. An abundance of salt-springs, coal-beds, and oil-wells induced respect for commerce and manufactures, and for mechanical and trading intelligence. A magnificent railroad, the work of Northern enterprise, in connecting the Ohio with the seaboard, unites West Virginia with both. The rivers of West Virginia rise and run their whole course within her own borders, and all flow into the free Ohio. The odd-shaped, prolonged district, squeezed between Ohio and Pennsylvania, and called the Pan-Handle, contains the busiest, most flourishing, and most intelligent town in the State, and is full of emigrants and the descendants of emigrants from New England, New York, and Pennsylvania. Thus shut off in her youth by bulwarks and fastnesses of nature's own engineering and handiwork from the blooming valley and fruitful plains of Old Virginia, and connected by rivers, railroad, community of interests, and congeniality of pursuits with the ready and enterprising North, it could not be that West Virginia should remain indissolubly attached to the East; and it is quite conceivable that even before the Secession movement the two portions of the State regarded each other with no friendly eyes.

Yet the new territory was proud of the grand old historical name; and the Old Dominion appreciated a region which has nowhere its superior, if its equal, in beauty, in grandeur, in variety, and in capacity for wealth.

These last and only ties the hand of loyalty was forced to cut. A Convention, representing the counties west of the Alleghanies, met at Wheeling after the passage of the Ordinance of Secession, and honestly carried out the wishes of the people. Consequently, twenty-nine counties of Virginia remained true to the United States Government.

These proceedings vastly increased the disgust of the old families of the East to the upstarts of the West, while they did not at all diminish their appreciation of the remunerative valleys and the tax-paying manufactories between the Ohio and the Alleghanies. They sent politicians to pursue diligently and cunningly the work of conversion, while they lost no time in preparing an army to take forcible possession.

It may be thought, from their loyalty, from their comparative enterprise, from the small number of their slaves, and from their freedom from the most vicious influences of slavery, that the West Virginians are a peculiarly intelligent people. On the contrary, while here and there are highly cultivated individuals and families, large numbers of the people are very ignorant, — victims of the hatred borne by the Southern States to free schools. At the taking of the last census, the Virginians unable to read were reckoned at a hundred thousand. The proportion of this number found in the Western valleys is not small. More than four fifths of the men arrested since the beginning of the war have been obliged to make their mark, in lieu of their names, to the oath of allegiance.

There is a region in Randolph and Webster counties, along the sources of the Cheat and the Holly, where are forests as savage as the unexplored wildernesses of Oregon. There the growl of the bear, the cry of the panther, and the bark of the wolf are sometimes still heard, and the dreary owl nightly wakes the echoes. Laurel-brakes stretch out like inland seas, and with never-fading leaves and snake-like branches interlaced, forbid a passage to even the light-footed deer; blackberry bushes extend miles in compact masses; superb firs lift up their crowned heads to the height of a hundred and fifty feet; and silvery cascades never cease their solitary murmur. Scattered wherever a clearing can most easily be made, in log-cabins, which bear a closer resemblance to wood-piles than to dwellings, live mountaineers to whom a newspaper is a curiosity, a book a sealed mystery, a locomotive an unimaginable monster, and a telegraph wire a supernatural agency, the touch of which might produce some indefinable evil. Even a tallow-candle is not a familiar thing, and a slip of pine lights the narrow precincts of the rude cabin, or pine knots send out from the wide chimney a glare more brilliant than the gas of cities.

A mountaineer, who had lived thirty years on one farm in this district, was asked by our scouts the name of his county. "Virginny!" he answered, and was positively unaware of the subdivision of a State into counties. Yet this man was in as good circumstances, and seemed as intelligent as his neighbors. At the same time an old woman, with imperturbable gravity, insisted that her family were neither Unionists nor Secessionists, but Baptists.

Even when education laid hold of the elementary sciences of reading and writing, it stopped short of grammar and orthography. Captured mail-bags exhibited curious and sometimes incomprehensible imitations of sound. Neither profanity nor treason are discoverable in a resolution to support the Secession cause " as shure as goddlemity ranes."

Ignorance tells more painfully upon women than upon men; and the women are listless, hopeless, sallow, lean, gaunt, and ugly beyond description. Were it not for a certain expression of sad patience on their face and in their demeanor, they could not but be objects of ridicule or disgust to the stranger. Their morbid imaginations have long received with ready credence the wild stories of Abolition cruelty passing from mouth to mouth, and they have been taught to regard Abolitionists as moral outlaws, violators of every social, civil, and divine ordinance. Secession agents found encouragement in every secluded valley, mountain forest, or mossy village, and had no difficulty in convincing even voters, that, in order to preserve the Union, it was necessary to crush Abolitionism, the bugbear which for the last thirty years has frightened the refractory into submission. A hundred young men, who joined Wise from one district, were fully persuaded that they were engaged in a crusade against Abolitionism, which was seeking the destruction of the Government. But it is a great and happy truth, that, while prejudice, suspicion, and hate find a genial soil in ignorant minds, the principles on which the good of humanity depends may be apprehended by the plainest understanding. We find many a man, to whom the alphabet is a mystery as occult as Egyptian hieroglyphics, looking straight at the right in this question of Secession and Union, recognizing his duty to the Government and disdaining disloyalty.

By the orders of the Confederate Government, General Garnett, about the middle of May, with a force of ten or twelve thousand, took possession of the gaps in the broken range west of the Alleghanies, called Cheat Mountains, and advancing along the turnpike, established his head-quarters at Beverly, a village on the eastern base of a long ridge parallel with the Alleghanies and the Cheat, and known as the Laurel Hill. From this point he sent detachments to various places in the valleys of the Tygart and the Cheat rivers. The detachment stationed at Grafton, which commands the railroad, in a little while destroyed the bridges in the direction of Wheeling. General McClellan, whose department included West Virginia, immediately ordered troops to advance into the disputed territory, and issued proclamations at the same time to his soldiers and to the inhabitants. He declared to the people that his army should respect property of every kind, in no way causing or allowing the institution of slavery, whether among loyal or disloyal owners, to be disturbed. His proclamation to the soldiers closed with the noble sentiment of mercy: "Soldiers, remember that your only foes are armed traitors, and show mercy even to them when in your power, for many of them are misguided." General McClellan was warmly seconded by his subordinate officers, and as warmly by the privates. Every man in the United States uniform, called to West Virginia, understood that mercy and justice were to go hand in hand, and had at the same time a proud satisfaction in marching to the relief of a gallant people threatened with destruction.

May 27th, the First Virginia, a regiment which was raised and offered to the President immediately after the Convention at Wheeling had resolved that the counties there represented should not secede, and two Ohio regiments, were ordered to drive the enemy from Grafton. After some delay, caused by the necessity of building bridges, they arrived to meet, instead of a warlike, an enthusiastically friendly reception. — The Rebel troops had retreated to Philippi.

## CHAPTER IV.

### GETTING INTO ACTION.

BEFORE Indiana's first brigade has entered upon its career of danger and duty, it may be well to form some acquaintance with the colonels, the men on whom, perhaps more than on any other, privates are dependent for health and comfort, for mental and moral improvement, for success in the day of battle and on the perilous march, and for safety when for safety the soldier may blamelessly strive; — and an introduction to Indiana's first Brigadier-General may not be amiss. They are all men in their prime, although Milroy, the oldest, bears in his gray hair and in the number of his years, fifty-five, tokens that he has passed the line we call the meridian of life; and Wallace, the youngest, does not yet count thirty-five, and in his buoyant step and lithe form gives no indication of the insinuating influences which in the maturity of years seldom fail to steal away the spring and gush of life.

THOMAS T. CRITTENDEN, Colonel of the Sixth, was born in Alabama, educated in Kentucky, and had his first experience as a lawyer in Missouri. In 1846, when war was declared between Mexico and the United States, he threw aside his books, left a lucrative and rapidly increasing practice, and enlisted as a private in the Second Regiment of Missouri Volunteers, then commanded by Colonel Sterling Price. He remained in the service until near the close of the war, received promotion to a lieutenancy, and was afterwards selected by his superior officers to write a history of the regiment. He became a citizen of Madison, Indiana, in 1848, and pursued the practice of law with energy and success. His Southern training gave him such an insight into Southern character and views, that, while almost every other individual in the State ridiculed the idea of rebellion, he acknowledged the danger, and endeavored to rouse a general anxiety. As early as January 1861, he organized a company and offered it to Governor Morton. On the 19th of April he went to Indianapolis with his company, and shortly after was elected and commissioned Colonel of the Sixth Regiment. Crittenden is stout and ruddy, frank, genial, and cheerful, with the comfortable, friendly aspect and manner which distinguish the Kentucky gentleman.

Colonel DUMONT, of the Seventh,—sallow, lean, and small, with an irascible, melancholy countenance, lighted up by a keen, deep-set eye, and sometimes additionally illuminated by flashes of dry humor,—is not only strikingly unlike the good-humored, hearty Crittenden, but is a sort of contrast within himself, and consequently has earned an unenviable reputation for eccentricity. Few men laugh so heartily, yet few look so morose; few are so tender, almost none so harsh; not many are so generous, yet many are more kind. He has attacks of devoutness which would lead one to think him most reverent and pious, yet his most partial friends do not call him religious. As lawyer, politician, and banker he has shown shrewdness, industry, and remarkable uprightness.

He was born in Indiana, in Vevay, a little Swiss town on the Ohio,—was taught principally by his mother, a woman of genius, who, if she had not been absorbed by the cares of a large family, and worn by the privations of a new country, would have won enduring fame as a writer,—and studied law with his father, a man also of ability, education, and refinement of feeling. Almost the first act of the son, however, on arriving at maturity, was to announce himself a Democrat in a public meeting, to the great disgust of the old Whig, his father, who immediately rose and stalked out of the house. Although not a man of military habits and tastes, and so under the influence of passing emotions that tactics and army discipline can be anything but agreeable, he volunteered even before the present war, and served honorably and usefully under General Taylor in Mexico. Such of the circumstances of war as touch a poetic fancy no doubt warmed his enthusiasm, but patriotism was the main incentive, and he then was as eager for the growth and glory of his country as he is now resolute for its preservation. He was prominent among the speakers the night of the announcement of the surrender of Sumter; and his eloquence, made up of mingled pathos, wit, and denunciation, and uttered in a voice so peculiar that it seemed to mock at his own feelings, drew tears and laughter and shouts from his excited audience. He led the list of offerings to the Government that night by the contribution of a horse with a man on his back.

Colonel MILROY, of the Ninth, is also a native of Indiana. His father was so strong a Democrat in theory and practice, that he had an unconquerable aversion to colleges, and obstinately refused the earnest entreaties of his son Robert to be allowed a liberal education,—entreaties to which the son added an offer to relinquish all claim upon the paternal estate. The boy was obliged to content himself with books at home, with which his father, with an inconsistent liberality, supplied him, until he was twenty-four years old; when, taking advantage of a visit to some relatives in Pennsylvania, he pursued his way to a military institution in Norwich, Vermont. A generous uncle gave him pecuniary assistance until the sturdy Democrat at home relented. In 1843 he graduated, taking the degrees of Master of Arts, Master of Military Science, and Master of Civil Engineering. He travelled several months in New England, teaching fencing and acquiring an acquaintance with Yankee landscape and character. In 1845 he went to Texas and took the oath of allegiance to the Lone Star, but after a few months returned to Indiana and settled down to the study of law. He was a captain in the First Indiana Regiment in the Mexican War, and when his term of service expired, endeavored unsuccessfully to procure the acceptance of himself, with a company of mounted infantry, to serve during the war,—making application first to General Taylor, afterwards to the Governor of Texas and the Secretary of War. Repeated refusals left nothing to the disappointed captain but to return home and continue the study of law. He attended lectures in Bloomington, received a degree, and was admitted to the bar in 1849.

Early in 1861 Milroy was convinced that war was inevitable, and February 7th issued a call for the formation of a volunteer company. Up to the fall of Sumter he succeeded in getting but two recruits: Gideon C. Moody, now captain in the Eighteenth Regulars and member of General Thomas's staff in the Army of the Cumberland; and Albert Guthridge, now captain in the Forty-eighth Indiana regiment. While it was still dark, on the morning after the announcement of the surrender, with the Court-House bell, a drum and fife, he roused and assembled the town of Rensselaer, his place of residence, and completed the number before breakfast. The same day he reported to Governor Morton in Indianapolis.

There is something in the majestic figure of ROBERT MILROY, in the erect head, held often as if watching or listening, in the fearless, restless eye, and gray hair turned back from the narrow forehead, so suggestive of the cognomen his soldiers have bestowed on him, that one is tempted to wonder why even in peace he was not called the "Gray Eagle."

LEWIS WALLACE is very American in appearance. His deep, flashing, black eye, straight, shining, black hair, and erect figure, would be no discredit to the haughtiest Aboriginal; and the boldness and sharpness, vigor and delicacy of his features, the insatiable yet controlled mental activity pervading the whole man, and still more the shade of sadness, tinged with scorn, resting on his face, and seeming to indicate a sort of self-pity, perhaps because of the contrast between the transitory nature of the goods of ambition or business, and the ardor employed in their pursuit, decidedly stamp him of the Anglo-American race, which, as a late English traveller says, "loses in the second generation all trace of European parentage," certainly the quiet and apparent stolidity of the genuine Englishman.

Lewis Wallace handles the pen and brush with ease and taste, and the lawyer's tongue, in his mouth, has lost none of its accredited skill. But his genius is military. The clash of arms enticed him, when he was scarcely past his boyhood, to the fields of Mexico; and the years spent in the exercise of his profession found their choicest recreation in the drill of a company of home-guards, to which he taught the manœuvres of Napoleon's Zouaves. Like Dumont, he was educated in the Whig party, of which his father was a prominent and able member, and adopted Democratic principles when he arrived at an age to vote. Colonel Wallace is a native of Indiana.

MAHLON D. MANSON, Colonel of the Tenth, was born in Ohio. He had few opportunities in his youth for intellectual cultivation, and is a self-made man, possessing that accuracy, ingenuity, independence, and self-satisfaction which he, who battles unaided with fortune and knowledge from his youth, is almost certain to acquire. He has spent the most of his life in mercantile pursuits; but he left the counter and the ledger in 1846 to engage in the Mexican War, and there received the instruction and the discipline which were to prepare him for a more responsible position in a more important conflict. In politics he was always an uncompromising Democrat. He is a solid, substantial, good-humored man in appearance, with very pleasant and popular manners.

WILLIAM P. BENTON was educated at Farmer's College, Ohio. He studied law early, and is a well-read lawyer. He showed his devotion to his country by sacrificing a large practice in the wealthy and pleasant town of Richmond to accept the charge of the Eighth. He is a safe, reliable man, unostentatious and earnest. He has the ruddy hue and rotund form of John Bull.

Indiana's first Brigadier-General is a man so quiet, so grave, so almost stolid in countenance and demeanor, with features so blunt, and coloring so dark and dead, that the eye of the observer, after resting with pleasure on the gallant, or animated, or thoughtful, or dignified colonels of his brigade, might turn to him with something like displeasure,— displeasure however to be swept away by a sure if slow recognition of the reserved power in the steady eye, of the gentleness and modesty eye and lip and life alike express. He stood high as a West Point student, being mentioned with honor in the report of the graduating class of 1834; and as a business-man, a gentleman, and a Christian, his reputation is unspotted. Indiana fondly and proudly speaks the name of THOMAS A. MORRIS, although his military history is suggestive only of him who is immortalized in the reflections of the royal misanthrope of Scripture,—the poor, wise man, who by his wisdom delivered a city, yet was remembered of none.

The Volunteers expected to be led off to battle, to a battle-ground at least, as soon as they enlisted; in consequence, they bore with extreme impatience the delay and the confinement and preparation in Camp Morton. Nothing was easier with their stalwart limbs and brawny fists than to fight; nothing harder to practise or endure than the monotonous manœuvres of dress-parade. Officers were not less impatient than privates, and earnest solicitations were forwarded to the President and General Scott for permission to move the Indiana forces toward the East. At length General Scott gave orders for the immediate removal of the Sixth, Seventh, and Ninth regiments to West Virginia. It is impossible to describe the delight afforded to the designated regiments by the announcement of these orders. The long tedium broken, the dull monotony dispelled, the door to action opened and the way made clear, life seemed to have a greatness hitherto unknown. The Volunteers felt that they were born for this day, and for the proud work of redeeming their country.

May 29th, the Seventh and the Ninth left Indianapolis. The Seventh was composed of men chiefly from the river counties. The Ninth was generally from the northwest. One of the privates in the latter regiment was a senator, and several were representatives in the legislature. May 30th, the Sixth followed. The Sixth was from the east and southeast counties; some Kentuckians, attracted perhaps by the name of Crittenden, one of their favorite statesmen and the old friend of their especial pride, Clay, had joined the standard of his nephew. It is said that one walked a hundred and twenty miles for the purpose. When the friends and relatives of the Volunteers in Madison were shaking hands and bidding good-bye, he said, sadly: "I've no one to say, 'God bless you!'" Instantly a hundred hands were extended, and a hundred "God bless you's" were uttered.

As fife-major in the Sixth went an unmusical young physician who had performed the duties of surgeon in camp, and had expected the position of assistant-surgeon in the field. But while he was practising in the hospital, somebody else practised in the Governor's mansion and obtained the place. Disappointed, but with undampened resolution, he applied to each regiment for admission as private, without being able to find a single vacancy. At last Colonel Crittenden kindly discovered that the Sixth was in need of a fife-major, and, without a very scrutinizing examination, introduced the applicant to the situation. The talents of the young doctor soon made his services in other quarters not only acceptable but needful, and he had but one march at the head of his regiment as fife-major.

On the route through Ohio, the troops met with welcoming honors, which would not have been inappropriate if bestowed upon returning victors. Dinners, breakfasts, and suppers were prepared for them; flowers were showered on them; speeches were made to them; ladies wept at the sight of them; old men with outstretched hands called down blessings upon them; infants were held above the heads of crowds to look at them. No act that rapturous enthusiasm could prompt was omitted.

The Ninth reached Grafton on the evening of the day on which the Ohio and Virginia troops arrived, and participated in the noise and joy of the welcome. The Seventh came the next morning; the Sixth was delayed by broken bridges, and Colonel Crittenden reached Webster, a few miles west of Grafton, not until the evening of June 2d. But four companies were with him, the remainder of the regiment having been left on the Ohio, to attack a little town where a muster of Rebels was reported.

From Grafton the Confederates had retreated to Philippi, a little town on Tygart's Valley River, and surrounded by hills capable of being easily and strongly fortified. With the policy of exaggeration they have never hesitated to pursue, they gave out, and their friends industriously spread the report, that their number amounted to not less than three thousand. It did not in reality exceed fifteen hundred. General Morris arrived at Grafton on the evening of June 1st, and found that Colonel Kelley had organized an expedition for that night against Philippi. After a full conference with Colonel Kelley, he deemed it advisable to postpone the attack until the following night. The next morning Colonel Kelley received orders to take six companies of his own regiment, nine companies of Colonel Milroy's, and six companies of Irvine's Sixteenth Ohio, to proceed on the railroad to a point six miles east of Grafton, and to march by the shortest and best route to Philippi. He must arrange his rest at night in such a manner that he could be sure of coming before the town at four o'clock next morning. Accordingly, at nine in the morning Colonel Kelley moved off in the direction of Harper's Ferry. The spies, who were numerous and active in Grafton, understood the movement to be against Harper's Ferry.

General Morris then organized another attacking column under Colonel Dumont. It consisted of eight companies of the Seventh, to be joined at Webster (a point a few miles southwest of Grafton) by five companies of Ohio Volunteers, commanded by Colonel Steedman, and two field-pieces, to be under the especial charge of Colonel Lander,\* who volunteered his services; also by four companies of the Sixth Indiana. They were directed to reach Philippi at precisely four o'clock. This column left Grafton after eight in the evening, and at Webster found the expected troops, Colonel Crittenden having just arrived from the west. The darkness was intense; rain poured down in torrents; mud was deep in the ravines, slippery on the hill-sides; the distance was twelve miles. Circumstances could not be more untoward. But it was the long desired moment for action, and the troops started out gayly. All night they trudged up-hill and down, drenched and dripping. The last five miles were made in one hour and a quarter. Many men fainted and were left on the road. Others threw away their haversacks and provisions, and with desperate exertions kept from falling behind. At daylight Colonel Dumont was heard shouting, "Close up, boys! Close up! If the enemy were to fire now, they couldn't hit one of you!" The order was well-timed; — the boys closed up and cheered up.

As they approached Philippi, they could perceive no evidences of the arrival of Kelley's detachment on the other side of the town. The infantry was ordered to halt, the artillery to advance and get the guns into position. Scarcely had this

\* Colonel Lander was Aid to General McClellan.

disposition been made when the pickets of the enemy commenced a brisk fire from the heights immediately above the town, and from the woods and bushes on both sides of the road. Colonel Lander opened fire. The pickets ceased. Nothing now obstructed the way. The troops waited a moment for orders; and as they waited, perhaps there was not a man whose eye did not glance with admiration upon the rare beauty of the scene spread below, — a green valley, encircled

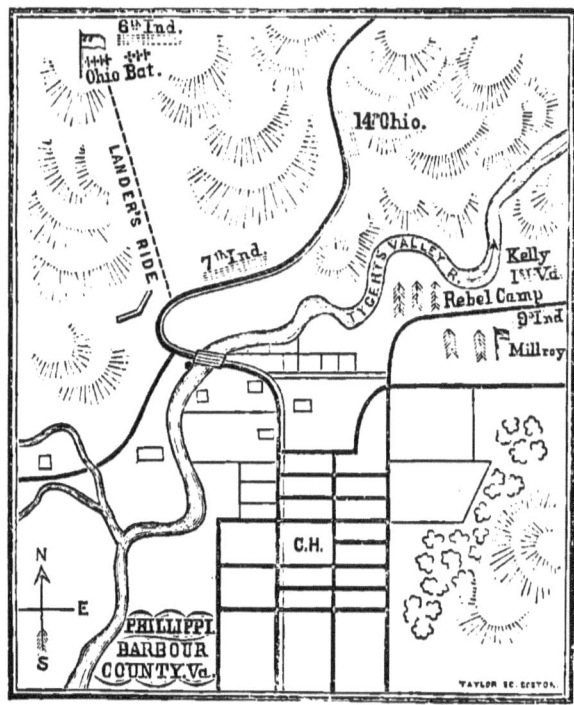

by forest-crowned cliffs and watered by a winding river, a little scattered village, and a snow-drift of tents on the dark sward. The pause was but momentary. With a wild, ringing cheer, the infantry, the Seventh in advance, rushed down the hill, through a narrow bridge, three or four hundred feet in length, which spans the river, dashing aside a barricade of boards as if it were of wicker, and poured on towards the Rebel camp. Unable to withstand the fascination of the shout and the race, the spirited, though moody, Lander left the artillery and urged his gallant gray down the rocky heights in front, with a temerity rivalling that of the old Putnam of Revolutionary times.

At this moment an answering shout was heard, and Colonels Kelley and Milroy were seen on the brow of the hill southeast of the town. In spite of a twenty-five mile march, the last few hours through mud and rain and darkness, down dashed the new-comers straight on to the Confederate camp. Unfortunately, their delay, though of not more than fifteen minutes' duration, left open one road. Toward this only door, out of the trap, without one attempt to get into line of battle, the whole body of Confederates turned face and foot.

"Great on a run, if not much for a fight!" muttered Colonel Dumont, as he reined in his horse and cast his eye over the scene.

Pell-mell, helter-skelter, without boots, without hats, without coats, without pantaloons, through the town, up the southern road, over the wall of hills, away they fled, incontinently, ingloriously, ignominiously. "Shirt-tail retreat!" No other thing with so mean a name ever inspired so glorious a pursuit. On, on came the Union troops, so tired an hour before they could scarcely lift their mud-encumbered feet, now fresh as pointers starting up the game. On they came, shouting and yelling, pell-mell, helter-skelter, up the height, down the height, and scattering through the wood. Peremptory orders at length recalled the unwearied Seventh, and stopped the ardent Ninth. The Sixth, too much fatigued to join in the pursuit, had quietly taken possession of the camp.

The immediate results of this affair were the capture of twenty-five thousand dollars' worth of goods, including a train, which had just arrived, with fifteen boxes of flint muskets; a number of banners, one of which was a splendid blue silk, presented by the ladies of Bath County two days before, and still redolent of exhortations to bravery and vows of fidelity;—killed to the number, it was supposed, of forty; a few prisoners; and such an inauguration of the campaign as greatly discouraged one side and proportionably encouraged the other.

One of the prisoners was taken in a somewhat singular manner. Some half-dozen soldiers were thrusting their sharp bayonets into a pile of hay, when a lawyer by the name of Martin, the private secretary of Colonel Porterfield, the Confederate commander, issued from under it in mortal terror. Assuming a composed and candid countenance, he declared that he had been thinking very seriously within the last few minutes about this secession movement, and was now ready to take the oath of allegiance. No Union soldier was killed, and but two wounded, — Colonel Kelley and a private.

More than three fourths of the inhabitants of Philippi had fled, but their property was scrupulously guarded. A beautiful watch, found in a hastily-vacated house, was returned to the owner, who was a lady, with the following note: —

" Our soldiers love and admire women. We come not to plunder, but to protect, and to crush rebellion. My kindest regards." Signed, " A soldier of the Ninth Reg. Ind. Vols."

The tidings of the affair of Philippi excited an interest in Indiana, as the first encounter, if encounter it could be called, with the Rebels, scarcely less intense than that produced later by the important battles of Stone River or Gettysburg, and penetrated with little delay to isolated farms and dwellings whither letters and newspapers seldom find their way.

One day in June, a lady with her family was slowly ascending one of those long, lonely hills which the Bloomington road through Morgan County so often climbs, when she was accosted by a pale, sad-looking woman, who asked for a newspaper. " I have none," said the traveller; " but why do you want a paper?" " I want to read about the battle of Philippi," answered the anxious woman; " I don't know the particulars yet, and I have two sons in the Seventh."

The traveller immediately gave the stranger a seat in her carriage, and as they drove leisurely along, related all she knew of the battle and of the regiment. In return, the country woman gave an account of her sons, how they were away from home at work on a neighbor's farm when the call for soldiers came. It was on a Saturday. The younger put his name down first. He was a good boy, but he was thoughtless; then, too, he had a weak chest, and who knew what he might have to bear of cold and hardship! So the elder, part for his country but part for his brother, enlisted too. He was twenty years old, steady and religious. She was not uneasy about him, nor about the younger either, for had n't he his brother to take care of him, and was n't it in a good cause? They did not come home Saturday nor Sunday; she reckoned they could not tell her; and they went away Monday without ever saying good-bye, — only in a letter which somebody brought her the same morning. From Indianapolis they sent her their " profile " ; and they wrote another letter, which the mother repeated word for word, beginning with the date, and ending with, " Yours till death."

" I wander around these hills," she said, " day and night, thinking about my two boys, for they are all I have, and wondering if they will ever come home again."

The travellers had now reached the woman's house, a little cabin, near a hazel thicket by the roadside, and they left her there; but many a time since they have recalled the plaintive voice and lonely wanderings of the soldiers' mother.

General Morris hoped to atone for the escape of the Confederate force from Philippi by resuming the pursuit, and continuing it until the enemy had either been defeated in battle, or driven beyond the mountains. But with a force of little more than six thousand, a large portion of which must guard the railroad and its two branches; with insufficient funds; without quartermaster or commissary; and under the necessity of giving a careful and impartial trial to numerous prisoners; it was impossible for him to make any movement. Assured that the troops in Camp Dennison and Camp Morton were suffering from inactivity and disappointment, he requested reinforcements. General McClellan, embarrassed by the want of wagon-trains and by his want of confidence in undisciplined Volunteers, felt it impossible to comply. Morris therefore continued at Grafton, and did all that was possible under the circumstances. Mounted scouts, few in number, but active and efficient, scoured the country in search of Rebel citizens and spies. Captain Tripp, of the Sixth, headed a particularly efficient body of scouts. Forces of fifty or a hundred were frequently sent to disperse parties gathered for. muster. Prisoners generally professed themselves willing to take the oath of allegiance; and they received without compunction the forgiveness of the lenient Government. They were also often the recipients of simple and earnest instruction in regard to their duty.

The Confederates were thoroughly dissatisfied with the inauguration of the campaign in West Virginia, but they saw with surprise and pleasure, and proceeded at once to take advantage of the enforced inactivity of the Federal troops. They brought reinforcements through the Cheat Mountain passes, and rapidly concentrated at Beverly and at Huttonville. In the Laurel Hill Range they built fortifications of great strength. The northern and principal, called Laurel Hill Camp, formed the head-quarters of General Garnett. The southern, under the command of Colonel Pegram, was established merely for the protection of Garnett's rear. The forest from one camp to the other, and stretching away along the mountains, was almost unbroken, and so dense that an army supplied with provisions might lie here months undiscovered. Even this wilderness was penetrated and its depths revealed by Morris's scouts: horsemen, where the thickets were accessible to horse; footmen, through every glade and glen, in every copse, on every rock, scanning the enemy's strength from overhanging cliffs, listening to the talk of Rebel sentinels, and entering the very precincts of the Rebel camp. The following narrative illustrates, better than any description of a third party, the danger, daring, and toil incident to a scouting expedition.

## SCOUTING.

#### NARRATIVE OF W. D. F.

June 27th, a man was wanted who would visit the Rebel camp at Laurel Hill Mountain, to get the position and number of the enemy, — also the fortifications, of which we had heard much from the country-people. I volunteered and was accepted by Colonel Dumont, then in command. I left head-

quarters at nine P. M., with a rough but honest specimen of Virginia backwoodsman for a guide, De Hart Wilson by name. His father was then a prisoner for Union expressions. We were clad in the guise of farmers. Colonel Crittenden furnished us with horses as far as Buckhannon Bridge, where we were to leave them with our scouts who were out on that road. The moon was bright. At eleven, two hours after we started, we were halted at a little church by our scouts. We asked for an escort as far as the bridge, but the officer in command refused it, saying the bridge was full of Rebels. One of his men rode up and said, "Captain, I will go with them to the bridge, and bring back their horses." "All right. If you were not an independent, I would not let you go. But don't go beyond the bridge with the horses."

The brave and kind offer of the stranger touched my heart. I had never before seen him. He had a well-worn hunting-shirt, belted about his waist with a raw-hide thong, from which hung a long duelling-pistol. An old felt hat, full of holes, was thrown on his head as if by chance, and seemed ready to fall off. His little black eye was sunken beneath a heavy eyebrow and a massive forehead. His black hair was cut short. His blacker moustache and beard were heavy, but neatly trimmed. Above all, his riding was peculiar, easy, and balanced as if he were part of his horse, and light and graceful as the swinging of a canary bird in the ring that hangs in its cage. He said not a word until we arrived at the long dark bridge. Here he stopped. "I am sorry; but my orders. Look out, friends. Enemy near. Lose your heads."

"Don't fear for us," said I, "the d—l take the hindmost!" "Good-bye! God bless you!" returned he. I felt queer at this from so rough-looking a man. "What's your name?" I asked. "Len' Clark," he answered, as he turned his horse toward Philippi.

Wilson and I crossed the bridge, and hurriedly pursued our way along the road, occasionally stopping to listen for Rebel scouts, but not speaking a word. The moon still shone, lighting up the gloomy arches of the forest. After walking six miles, we left the road, and without pausing took a western course through the wilderness. On we went, in pathless woods, through ravines tangled with azalea, whose perfume hung heavy on the midnight air; up the craggy mountain-side, saturated to the skin with cold dew; on through the laurel thicket, scaring the whippoorwill from his home; over the mossy trunks of fallen forests; down the steep bluffs; wading cold streams; on we went all night long. Near morning the guide hesitated, and at length acknowledged that we were out of our course. We threw ourselves down on the pine logs, and took an hour's rest.

Just at daybreak we heard a cock crow, and following the direction of the shrill clarion, we found a little farm-house. We roused the frightened farmer, and Wilson inquired the direction to Coon Carpenter's. We learned the course and were off at full speed, for Coon Carpenter was a Union man, and it was necessary to reach his house before sunrise. In passing over a farm, two men saw us, and immediately hid themselves in the woods. The Rebel camp was within seven miles of us, and the people who professed Union sentiments were very shy, sleeping in the woods in the daytime, and only at night daring to come out of their mountain hiding-places to visit their families. Everybody was suspicious of strangers.

We crossed the farm of an old Dutchman, by the name of Rohrbach, and, wanting further information, we concluded to make a halt at the rear of his cabin. Two half-black, half-yellow, half-starved Virginia 'coon dogs came at us. Their barking brought Mrs. Rohrbach to the door, where she took up a position she seemed inclined to keep, while she with frightened look surveyed us. She was six feet long, with an ugly, angular face, the color of putty. Her nose was long and thin. Her mouth was like a gash in a frost-bitten squash; flopping open, it revealed three long front teeth, blackened with smoke and calomel. On each temple were three little, flat, blue-colored curls, which seemed to have been made and put there under the pressure of a ton to the inch. She had no other hair or hairs on her head. A black clay pipe, with a long cane stem, was held tightly, upside-down, between her snags. Her eyes resembled two large pewter buttons, dipped in lard. Her frame was the only thing she retained of what may once have been a good-sized body. I describe Mrs. Rohrbach so minutely, because she is rather a type of a West Virginia wife at middle age. We asked for her husband; she answered, interrogatively: " I reckon you don't want to hurt him ? " We didn't wish to hurt him. She pointed to a field with her long, bony finger, and there we soon found Rohrbach. He was a quiet old Dutchman, as ugly as his wife, whom, he said, he married for "use, not looks." It was now only half-past four in the morning, and he had been ploughing some four hours by moonlight, with his oldest boy. Two smaller tow-heads, dressed in dirty homespun shirts and ragged pants, were stationed on the fence at either end of the field, to tell the old man if any Rebels or strangers were approaching, when he would make tracks for the woods.

After some conversation, in which we learned that the road to Carpenter's was scouted by the Rebels, and that they had been at his house last night, we proceeded with caution on our journey, and arrived within an hour at Coon Carpenter's. Coon lived five miles from his nearest neighbor. His farm is a specimen of the middle class of Virginia farms. It is a small opening in the forest, from which the trees have been " deadened," and is secluded from all the world. A few acres of Virginia wheat, a few of corn, and a tobacco patch, are surrounded by a rickety rail-fence, in the corners of which weeds most do flourish. Another space, fenced in and called the "Dead'nin," is used to pasture two or three old horses; one or two colts; mane and tail matted with burs; half a dozen sheep; and a cow. A few long, land-pike, blue pigs run at large. The cabin of Coon is, like all Virginia cabins, composed of rough logs, sticks, pins, and mud.* Inside are two huge feather beds, under which are a trundle-bed, boxes, and all the odds and ends of the establishment. The window (there is not always a window in these mountain cabins) is small; the fireplace large. A gun-rack, made of antlers, is over the door. A shelf of rough boards supports the meagre store of blue or red china.

* Many of the backwoods cabins are built without the use of iron fastenings, such as nails, screws, &c.

Coon Carpenter and son are both Union men. Coon is tall, and about fifty years of age. His son much like him, and half his father in years. Both were barefooted, unwashed, homespun men. Not a member of the family can read or write, and no books or papers are seen about this primitive house. The boy calls the father "dad," and the man calls the boy "sonny." The mother and daughters are wild, shy people, say nothing, but stare suspiciously. Women never enter into conversation, in the company of strangers, and never sit at the table with them.

We took breakfast, ham and ash-cakes, and after procuring some tobacco, completed our journey in another five miles, making a distance of thirty-five miles in ten hours, including the rests. We were now a mile and a half from the Rebel camp, at the house of Mr. Stephens, a good and remarkably shrewd Union man; and Wilson left me to visit his mother, who lived some two miles north. Mrs. Stephens called her two little boys from the cornfield, and directed them to keep a sharp lookout. If they saw any one coming, they were to whistle, but not to run to the house. She sent two wild-looking girls to watch from a neighboring hill. They were to pretend to pick strawberries, and if they saw any of the Rebels coming over the river, they were ordered to walk slowly homeward. After these directions were given, I was shown to an old gum,* into which I crawled. Overcome with fatigue, I soon fell asleep. At three P. M. I awoke refreshed, but sore from my hard journey. My guide had not returned, neither had Stephens, who was hid in the woods; so, after eating some corn-bread and wild honey, I started with a little boy seven years old as a guide to Wilson's house. We were obliged to keep in the woods, away from all paths, for fear of meeting strolling parties of Rebels. Such a thing as a wagon-road could not be found on that side of the Beverly pike. A slight fall of rain had made the leaves damp, and we could walk with less danger of attracting attention, which was important, as we were now within the line of the Rebel pickets. I noticed that my little guide broke twigs from the

* A section of a hollow tree, as large in circumference as a hogshead, but higher, used by country people to put grain in, or to stow away meat.

overhanging boughs to mark the way, so that on his return he might not get lost. He left me near the home of Wilson, which was a very good double log cabin. I climbed into a service-tree, and gave the signal we had agreed upon: three deep, hollow hoots like an owl. An answer came from the woods back of me. It was well for me that I did not approach the house, for in it was a company of Rebel officers at dinner. Wilson had fled at their approach, and was hid in the woods, waiting their departure.

It was growing late, and we went off through the valley to the east, and climbed a bluff on the banks of Valley River, from the top of which I could look into the Rebel camp. I saw tents and horses and men,—men drilling, men working; I saw rifle-pits and fortifications, on which I could distinguish guns mounted; and I saw the flag, the stranger and traitor to my soil, flaunting freely in the mountain-breeze. Now, first, did I realize that war existed in my own country.

My guide left me to make observations, and to keep watch. He was to come back at sunset. The Rebel camp was perhaps five hundred yards in a direct line below and to the east. The rain caused a fog in the valley, and put an end to my observations for the night; so I returned to the woods below, hooting occasionally, but getting no reply. It now began to rain very hard, and grew quite dark. I took shelter on the dry side of a leaning oak, not far from a bridle-path, and sat quietly listening to that lonesome mountain warbler, the wailing whippoorwill, whose notes send a peculiar thrill through the heart of the wandering scout. Soon I heard the tramp of a horse; nearer, the occasional clank of a sabre; nearer still, voices: "I say, Sergeant, this is a wild-goose chase. Hart Wilson left these parts more than a week ago." "We are in for a wetting to-night." "No danger of Yanks along these roads, anyhow."

Soon the sounds grew indistinct and died away altogether in the valley below. Six Rebel horsemen had passed within ten steps of me. I feared they might find Wilson at home, for they hated and dreaded him; and I renewed my hooting. No answer but the dropping rain on the thick roof of leaves overhead. I started off in the dark, forded the river up to my arms, and followed up a little creek till in full view of the smouldering camp-fires. I could hear the sentinels, relief-guards, whistling and laughing at the guard-house. I could see a light in the house, Mustoe's, which I supposed was used as a hospital. I was about to go nearer, when a sentinel passed me, yawned, and struck his musket on the ground.

This trip cost me many hours, and brought me nothing; for although almost in among their tents, I could see nothing of importance, and it took me until daylight to get back to the cliff. In the early dawn I found my way to Wilson's, and hooted him out. He invited me in, saying that he was hid near the house till two A. M.; that from the action of his dogs he thought some one was watching him, but when day dawned he found the coast clear. I went in, took some breakfast, and was soon sound asleep; but, for the first time in my life, in a cellar!

At nine A. M. I went once more to the bluff, climbed a tree, and made drawings of the camp and country. At half-past ten started with my guide to Coon Carpenter's, where we found that the Rebels were on our track. We also learned from a Rebel woman, who had been through the camp that morning, as she came from mill, that a train of a hundred wagons had started on the Moorefield road for corn. We made ourselves good Rébels to our informant, and she appealed to us to confirm the news she was telling to Mrs. Coon and her daughters, evidently thinking we were just from camp. Coon was away: so was his son,— hid, I suppose.

Wilson and I now started by a new route to Philippi, on the double-quick. Seeing Rebels on our road, we followed down the Valley River, frequently crossing it. The way was very rough. My clothing hung in tatters. My feet were very sore. When within six miles of camp, I procured a horse, and leaving Wilson, arrived in camp at ten P. M., and reported to Captain Benham, U. S. E., and General Morris, who had arrived the day before from Grafton. I was forty-eight hours on this trip, and marched over sixty-five miles, with little sleep and food.

General Morris sent Major Gordon with despatches, and

me to report in person, to the Commanding General at Buckhannon. We started with an escort of six, led by the man who had taken my horse, and bidden me God-speed at the bridge, — Len' Clark, with his deep, intelligent eye peering from beneath his ragged hat. We arrived at Buckhannon without accident, just as the Major-General, with his splendid troops, was entering. Colonel Lander received the despatches

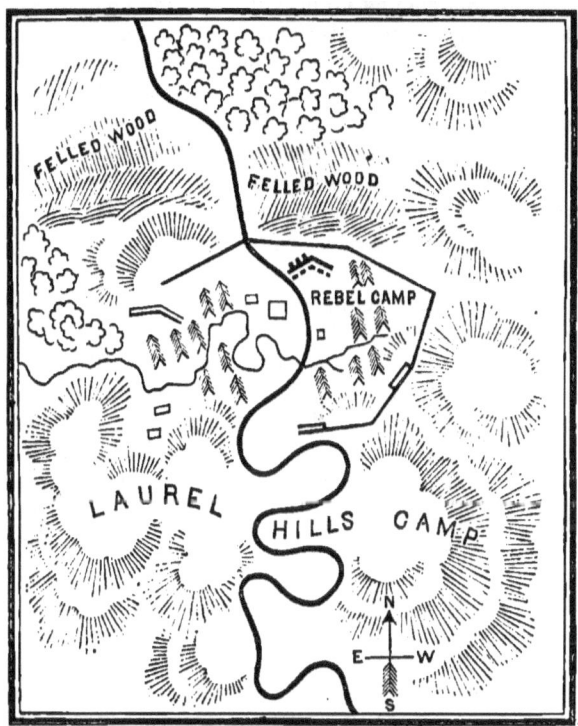

for General McClellan, and, while we were eating dinner at the hotel, came for me. We rode to a fine undulating plain, south of the town, where head-quarters were situated, and I was introduced to the little General. He was dressed in a fatigue-cap, a loose blouse, without marks of office, and light-blue pants. He was covered with dust, and was sitting at a little camp-table, on which was a topographical map of Virginia. He looked at me from head to foot before he spoke; then asked every particular in regard to my visit to the Rebel camp, the names of persons whom I met, the route, the hills, trees, streams, &c. I drew for him on a sheet of paper a map of the Confederate camp.*

After I had left the General's tent, a brisk, pleasant little man began talking with me, and seemed very much interested in all I had to say. I supposed him to be a quartermaster, but Col. Lander coming up introduced me to Gen. Rosecrans. — Here for the present ends the narrative of the Scout.

General McClellan had assumed command in person in West Virginia on June 21st. His head-quarters were first at the venerable and sleepy town of Clarksburg, but removed in a few days to Buckhannon, with the intention of advancing from this point to the rear of the fortifications on Laurel Mountains, at the western base of which the village of Buckhannon lies.

The Eighth and Tenth regiments, the former from the eastern, the latter from the western counties of Indiana, after two months in camp, left Indianapolis the 19th of June to repair to West Virginia. The train containing the Eighth stopped at North Bend, on the Ohio, and the aged widow of the brave old warrior and true-hearted President, whose name is dear to the nation, most dear to the West, advanced to the roadside to meet her grandson, Irwin Harrison, the adjutant of the regiment. As the young man bent before the frail, bowed woman, while with trembling voice she invoked heaven's richest blessings upon him, and upon all her country's defenders, it almost seemed that the dead lips of a buried generation said, Amen!

The cars were crowded and uncomfortable, but the enthusiasm of the people, and the beauty of the scenery in Virginia, — where men were reaping barley and ploughing corn by the roadside and on the hill-sides, and where long and high bridges, tunnels, grades, valleys, and mountains form a succession of picturesque landscapes, — more than compensated. The troops reached Clarksburg at six in the evening, and encamped in the rear of the town, in an almost impregnable

* See preceding page.

position, on a bold hill which commands a circuit of three miles.

There was a rumor afloat that Governor Wise, with an army somewhere between ten and fifty thousand strong, was approaching, and the newly arrived regiments were roused at two in the morning to work upon fortifications. In eight hours a breastwork from four to six feet high was thrown up on the north, east, and south sides, and a half acre of timber felled on the west. But instead of Governor Wise came a despatch from McClellan the next day, ordering an immediate march to Buckhannon. Tents had not yet arrived, but in a half-hour the troops were on their way. That night and the next they lay on the ground in the drenching rain, without any kind of shelter, and received thus their introduction into the hardships of the soldier's life, and their first lesson in the art of grumbling, — the soldier's peculiar and inalienable prerogative. An army, numbering twelve thousand, was now assembled at Buckhannon, and preparations for a speedy attack were unceasing and vigorous.

Meanwhile, the policy of forbearance was adhered to with undeviating resolution. The case of Symmes, the man who shot Colonel Kelley at Philippi, is but a fair example. Colonel Lander struck up the weapons pointed at him by the enraged Virginians of Kelley's command, and thus saved his life. He was allowed to board at the best hotel in Grafton, and to be quite unmolested in the enjoyment of a slightly circumscribed freedom. Avowed and active secessionists, even spies, were repeatedly released with no security for the future. In return, the most murderous and savage warfare was kept up by the enemy. Every forest, gorge, and thicket teemed with lurking foes, who fired without a challenge.

## CHAPTER V.

### LAUREL HILL, AND RICH MOUNTAIN.

THE Sixth, Seventh, and Ninth, with the associated Ohio and Virginia regiments, lay five weeks at Philippi and along the road to Grafton, idly waiting, while the Rebel troops continued industriously to fortify. The impatience of the soldiers in the preparatory camps was slight in comparison with the impatience of the troops now in the field. They burned with desire for action. They raged against McClellan, because he was weeks at Cincinnati, weeks at Clarksburg, and weeks at Buckhannon, and because his orders were always, *to wait.* But one day, as fretting and fuming they were scattered through the shady grove in which they were encamped, they heard the sound of firing in the direction of the enemy, whose outposts were at the little village of Bealington. At first, here and there; then, thicker and faster. " The Rebels are on us!" " The Rebels are on us!" A cry of joy, a rush to arms, a call to order, and almost instantaneously the line of battle was formed. There was Morris, calm and grave as usual; Love, all animation; Milroy, his eyes shooting fire; Dumont, haggard and ghastly, his uniform put on him by unwilling physicians, tottering to his horse, but now sitting firmly, steadily surveying his command, and saying with spirit: " Let them come; we are ready!" Virginia and Ohio were ready, too. But where was Crittenden? Where was the gallant Sixth? Surely the sound of firing ought to rouse them from the sleep of death! As the question ran from man to man, a reconnoitring party sent out by the General returned with the information that Colonel Crittenden's regiment was drilling on the Bealington road, and at this moment was engaged in a mimic battle. Deep as had always been the disgust of the loyal troops towards the Rebels, it never was so intense as at this moment, when, chagrined and crestfallen, they dispersed to their tents.

At this time, and indeed during the whole year in West Virginia, men were seldom or never detailed for a hazardous duty, unless volunteers were so numerous it was necessary to restrict the number. When a party was ordered to the execution of some undertaking, it was not unusual to find in the ranks double the proper number, — to find Company A, for instance, counting two hundred instead of one, and each man of the two hundred bearing in his countenance, if not on his tongue, an assertion that he was in his proper place.

Colonel Dumont was ill during the greater part of the stay at Philippi, — so ill that at one time alarm was felt, and his officers urged him to be removed to Grafton, where he could be comfortably accommodated. Stretched out on his camp-cot, with no luxury, not even a comfort about him, the suffering man replied: " No, never! When my boys get sick they lie here, and, if it must be, die at their posts. They don't get off, and I won't go, either."

July 6th, the President's Message was received, and the hearts of the Volunteers, as by the light of the setting sun they read that manly, honest document, responded to the great heart which throbbed in the breast of the ruler and leader of the nation. That night, when they wrapped themselves in their blankets, and lay down on their hard beds, within them glowed the purpose and the enthusiasm which lofty thoughts kindle, and which make the soldier's pallet nobler than the king's couch.

Before many hours, the sleeping camp was aroused, and midnight saw the long hoped-for march to Laurel Hill begin. The Ninth, preceded and flanked by skirmishers, formed the van. In order followed the Fourteenth Ohio, Cleveland Artillery, First Virginia, Seventh Indiana, Body-Guard, General and staff, three companies of the Sixteenth Ohio, Sixth Indiana, and Guthrie Grays, — about five thousand in all. Not a word was spoken, except of command, and not a sound broke the silence of the night, but the rumbling of wheels, and the steady, rapid tramp, tramp, of the troops. As the thousands of glimmering camp-fires died away in the distance, a misty moonlight half revealed and half concealed the dangers of the winding road, the threatening forests, the frowning rocks, and the ravines and gorges in which a thousand men might hide. Day lighted up the shaggy woods, and rugged cliffs, and discovered the blushing laurel and the bright azalea. Vigilance did not relax. The woods were scoured, the rocks explored, the army halted, while the treacherous turns of the crooked road were examined. The mountain farms were deserted, the houses closed, and no signs of life were visible, except now and then an anxious face peering through a curtained window. About half-past seven the enemy's pickets first seemed aware of the approach of our troops. They fired, but immediately fled. Just as the last were driven in, our army came in full view of the position to be occupied. In less than an hour it was successfully disposed on heights, which hemmed in the enemy, and General Morris had established his head-quarters in the house of Elliott, a noted Secessionist, who looked on with trembling rage, while the Stars and Stripes were placed above his unworthy door. In this prefatory skirmish, a private in the Ninth, William T. Girard, was killed.

Garnett's camp was hidden by two conical eminences, which, being densely wooded, furnished a fine cover for skirmishing purposes. It extended over about a hundred and fifty acres, and had a fine position, with a mountain wall behind it as a background and a shelter. General McClellan had already advanced from Buckhannon, and he issued orders to Morris, by all means to avoid an engagement, until the heavy column should appear in the rear. Whatever General Morris's long-tried patience, his troops had no inclination to employ themselves in the culture of a passive virtue, and they engaged in skirmishing with a zeal that threatened to anticipate McClellan's movements. Feats were daily performed, which, years from now, when veterans repeat tales of their youth to eager listeners, will thrill many a shuddering fireside.

Sylvester Brown, a tall private of the Sixth, in the face of six Rebels, who were behind an earthwork of rude construction, carried from a tree, where they had been cooking and resting, a quantity of blankets and some cooking-utensils. Placing them safely, he returned; but, as he was again carrying a parcel of blankets away, the Rebels stood up, took deliberate aim, and fired. He wheeled around, fired with steady hand, and stepping proudly and firmly as on dress-parade, reached his comrades, who surrounded him with offers of assistance. "I am shot," he said, "but the cowards don't know it!" and he would not be moved down to the hospital, lest they should see that he was wounded.

West of the Staunton turnpike, and not far from the Rebel works, was an old field, with here and there a clump of black-berries, a group of dead trees, or a pile of logs. On the east was a dense wood, with an undergrowth of laurel. One day field and wood were alive with skirmishers. In the wood the Rebels were comparatively safe, but our soldiers in the field must creep stealthily from log to tree, and from tree to bush, take aim with keen glance and rapid hand. A youth, with delicate face and form and light curling hair, lay behind a log near the road. He had in his hand a revolver, which he had taken from a dead Rebel officer the day before. Restless and impatient, he determined to cross the road and penetrate the dangerous wood. With swift step he put the thought into execution, cleared the road, hid in the thicket. A few minutes, and two shots were fired; then on the evening air rose a scream, so awful that no man who heard it will forget it to his dying day. Mortal agony was in that shrill cry. The skirmishers in the field sprang to their feet, and drew instantly together. The hasty and perilous resolve was made to dash into the wood. In the laurel, a few steps from the road, they found the bleeding, lifeless body of the reckless boy. He was John Auten, of the Ninth.

The hill known as Girard Hill, was taken from a regiment of Georgians, by fifteen privates without any officers. In the attack, two soldiers, Bierce and Boothroyd, advanced within fifteen paces of the enemy's fortifications, and here Boothroyd received a wound in the neck, which paralyzed him. His comrade immediately caught him in his arms and carried him and his gun full twenty rods, bullets falling around them at every step.

In the afternoon of the 10th of July, two large bodies of troops were seen from a high hill in the neighborhood, leaving the Rebel camp. Instant preparations were made to meet them, and in less than two hours the Fourteenth Ohio and Ninth Indiana were actively engaged with twelve hundred Georgians. The Rebels came forward under cover of the woods, holding their cavalry ready to charge whenever our men should attempt to move in anything like military order. Suddenly the Federals advanced, and poured in a sharp volley. The Rebel cavalry, taking advantage of the movement, proceeded to take them in flank. The Federals rapidly retreated, and, as they retreated, threw out a couple of shells. In their turn, the Confederates drew back, shouting, " Now, give it to them!" and springing forward at the same time, the Federals poured in another volley. The enemy wavered and fell further back, but recovered in a moment and dashed forward.

"Rally to your logs!" was now the cry of the Federals, and back they fled behind trees and logs and blackberry bushes. Shells were again thrown among the assailants, and again they fled to their sheltering woods. The Ohio and Indiana boys broke cover, and forward they dashed once more. Further, further they went until Milroy, who had charge of a gun, sprang upon a log and shouted, waving his hat, "Fall back, boys! We're going to fire another shell!" He stood several minutes, his head inclined, listening intently. At length through the tumult he distinguished the shout from his boys: "Fire more to the right!" The enemy scattered before this well-directed shell, and could not again be rallied.

"What troops are you?" it is said a Georgian shouted from behind a tree before any shells were thrown. "Ohio and Indiana Volunteers," was shouted in reply. "Can't make me believe that," called out the Georgian. "You need n't tell me that Volunteers stand fire that way." He was probably convinced they were Volunteers when he heard them, if through the din he could hear, singing out their own orders: "Now give it to them!" "Rally to your logs!" and the like.

John R. Smith, a young, brave fellow, who had walked thirty miles to volunteer, fell in this skirmish.

Milroy's men, like their leader, were madly in love with danger. It is said that one of them took a newspaper, and marching up the road at the foot of the hill, asked the Rebels if they would n't like to hear the news. "Yes!" they shouted. He unfolded his paper and began: "Great battle at Manassas Gap: one thousand Rebels killed; ten thousand wounded; nearly all the rest taken prisoners. All traitors to be hung, and their property confiscated." Here the bullets began to hail around him, and he beat a retreat.

It was almost impossible to restrain our men from making an assault that night. They had no longer expectation or hope of hearing the booming of McClellan's guns the other side of Laurel Hill. The next day they were early on the alert, eager at every point for skirmishing; but the enemy could not be induced to show himself. Not a gun was seen or heard, while the blows of the axe and the crash of falling timber never ceased. It was surmised that General Garnett had determined to make a last stand here, and was strengthening his intrenchments. Early the following morning, a horseman, without saddle, whip, or spurs, beating his horse on with his sword, came galloping to head-quarters, and announced that the Rebels had evacuated.

Intelligence so contrary to expectation and so disagreeable was received with suspicion, and General Morris ordered three officers, Captain Benham, Sergeant-Major Gordon, and Dr. Fletcher, with a company, to inspect. He also sent orders to Colonels Dumont and Milroy to march without a moment's delay to the enemy's camp. In five minutes both regiments were on the march. Along the smooth mountain road, past the blackberry field, and around the wooded knoll, they went, expecting to meet an open, or to hear an ambushed foe. Uninformed of the reported evacuation, their surprise and suspicion increased with every step. Not with fear, but with some trepidation, they looked towards a turn in the road before them, which might expose them to the raking fire of the enemy's cannon; but instead of bristling guns, the turn revealed a long line of unmanned intrenchments, silent batteries, and deserted tents.

"Where are General Garnett and his men?" asked Dr. Fletcher, who was first to cross the Rebel intrenchments, of a frightened woman in a solitary house. "They's done gone," she said.

He went into an old log house on Mustoe's farm, and found some eight or ten wounded Rebels. They handed him a note addressed to "Any officer of the U. S.," asking that mercy be shown to these wounded men. The men themselves begged him not to have them hung!

The Seventh and Ninth were joined at the camp by two companies of Ohio artillery, under Colonel Barnett, and pushed forward on the road to Beverly. It was now evident that the felling of trees, the day before supposed to be for the purpose of strengthening the intrenchments, was the work of the rear-guard, to delay pursuit. The road was blocked up with every possible obstacle, and strewed with the effects of the Rebels. The pursuit was continued ten miles, without further interruption than was necessary to drag trees out of the road; but at Leeds Creek was brought to an abrupt halt, by the want of a bridge, which the Rebels had broken up. While the bridge was undergoing repairs, a foraging party was sent out to obtain food from the neighboring farmers; but it returned with such a scanty supply, that even after one or two provision-wagons came up, many a man was unable to obtain a morsel. Near night the Fourteenth Ohio arrived. The advance was commanded by Captain Benham, U. S. E., one of those unfortunate individuals who have a peculiar facility for winning dislike; but not hunger, fatigue, nor Benham could cool the ardor of the troops, and they lay down on the ground to sleep with the utmost satisfaction.

General Morris arrived at Leeds Creek some time after dark, and was led among the sleeping forms of tired soldiers to an old log house, in which Captain Benham directed him by his voice, as no light could be obtained. The members of the staff lay on the ground, with the other soldiers, and endured a pelting rain.

Meantime events were occurring at Rich Mountain, which changed the course of the retreat, and consequently of the pursuit. At three o'clock on the morning of the 12th, the same morning Morris started in pursuit of Garnett, General Rosecrans, with the Eighth, Tenth, Thirteenth Indiana, and Nineteenth Ohio, left McClellan's camp west of Rich Moun-

tain, and proceeded along the line of hills southeast of the
enemy's intrenchments, with the purpose of entering the Beverly road on the mountain-top, and of attacking the camp
from the east. General McClellan was to assault the west
as soon as the firing should announce the commencement
of the attack.

General Rosecrans occupied about nine hours in cutting
his way through the woods, climbing the rocks, logs, and
stumps, and wading the streams. The guide was David
Hart, whose father's farm was on the top of the mountain,
and who had escaped from the Rebels by this route. Colonel
Lander, who had spent the greater part of his life in exploring and engineering expeditions in the far West, and whose
experience in military, mountain, backwoods, and every variety of wild, adventurous, and exposed life, was unusual,
accompanied the guide, and declared the difficulties of the
march unequalled. The bushes were wet, the air was excessively cold and full of rain; and rain began to fall in
the course of the morning. About noon they reached the
top of the mountain, but instead of descending and quietly
taking possession of the Rebel rear, according to the plan, they
were here saluted by a volley from Rebel pickets, whose attack
was followed by cannon; and they found themselves in the
presence of a large body of the enemy. A courier, sent by
McClellan to Rosecrans, had taken the broad Beverly road
which led directly through the Confederate camp, and had
of course been obliged to give up his despatches. In consequence, a body of twenty-five hundred men, with three cannon, had been sent to the top of the mountain, and had there
thrown up hastily some intrenchments.

Rosecrans made an attempt to form his command into
line, but it was found impossible, on account of the irregularities of the position; the troops were therefore ordered to
advance at intervals and fire; then throw themselves on the
ground. The Confederates fired steadily and rapidly, but the
screen of bushes prevented their taking correct aim, and they
fired generally too low. General Rosecrans attempted again
to form the troops into line, and after much difficulty, resulting partly from the nature of the ground, partly from the rain

which was now pouring down, and partly from the eagerness of the men to rush pell-mell into battle, he finally succeeded. The Eighth was ordered to take the right, the Tenth the centre, one half of the Thirteenth (the other half had been stationed at the forks of a road in the rear, with instructions to hold the point at all hazards) the left. The Ohio regiment was the reserve. The Thirteenth immediately advanced some distance to the left and down the hill, to flank the enemy. While directing its movements, Colonel Sullivan suddenly found himself face to face with a Rebel of immense size. The Colonel raised his sword and the Rebel his rifle. The sword bent and the rifle missed, but the Colonel's face was burned with the flash; and if one of his soldiers had not seen his danger, shoved him aside, and brought the Rebel to the ground, his first battle would probably have been his last. Some delay was occasioned by the Tenth, under a misapprehension of orders, taking the right. It marched down to within three hundred yards of the enemy, and engaged him hotly for thirty minutes, unassisted by the Eighth, which, the mistake having been discovered, was ordered to face about and march to the right. Both regiments showed great steadiness in march, countermarch, and actual battle.

At length the three regiments fell back, and the reserve was ordered forward. It advanced to a fence in line with the breastworks, fired one round, then gave three cheers to the Indiana boys, who fixed their bayonets with a clang which resounded along the lines, and rushed forward to charge bayonets. One man alone of the enemy stood his ground. He coolly touched the match to his cannon, at the same moment received a ball in his heart, and fell dead.

A general race now followed, so exciting that our men were with difficulty recalled and reformed in line of battle, to receive the enemy from the foot of the mountain. But instead of following up the attack, the Confederates, as well in the camp as on the top of the mountain, thought all was lost, and sought safety in the woods, leaving their works, tents, stores, cannon, and indeed all they had. The engagement lasted over an hour. On the battle-field was found a sword, inscribed with the testimony of the gratitude of the

State of Virginia to Midshipman Taylor, for his valorous defence, on two occasions, of a United States frigate.

General Rosecrans was very conspicuous in this battle. He was as cool and skilful as he was brave, and no higher praise of his bravery can be given than to say it equalled that of his men. They were all as brave as lions, but inclined to be regardless of orders, unless accompanied by a rap with the flat side of the sword. Even wounds did not quench or cool their ardor; more than one man with a disabled leg crawled to a stone and loaded for a comrade, or himself continued firing. The only banner in the engagement was that of the Eighth, the motto of which was: "ABOVE US OR AROUND US."

The next day, after thirty-six hours' wandering in the woods through rain and mud, without rest and without food, Colonel Pegram and about six hundred of his command surrendered themselves prisoners of war. They formed a melancholy procession. Colonel Pegram wore an expression of the deepest sadness, and the forlorn young faces of many students from Hampden Sydney College appealed to the hearts of the victors. The captain of the students was one of their professors. Did he feel shame, or is that last safeguard of the soul lost to the traitor?

On the day of Pegram's surrender, General Garnett was within three miles of Beverly, on his way either to unite his force — which at the outset of his retreat numbered five thousand, — with that of Pegram, and then to give battle, or to proceed for greater security to the fastnesses of the Cheat Mountains. When he received the unwelcome intelligence, he turned and retraced his march to Leeds Creek, from which point a mountain-road leads northeast through the little town of New Interest, to St. George, Tucker County. He entered this road early in the morning. The rain fell and continued to fall in torrents, making a deep, sticky mud of the clay soil, which the feet of the fugitives worked thin, and left rolling down the hills after them in sluggish streams. Proofs of their fatigue and of the lessening distance between them and their pursuers became more and more numerous to the latter. Knapsacks, trunks, clothes, beds, cards, everything that could be thrown away, marked the route. Rebel axes forming' barricades, and loyal axes, clearing away obstructions, answered to each other. Rebel pickets protecting laborers were driven in. A Rebel banner was taken, and borne back along the whole line. Every step increased the exhilaration of the National troops. As they waded a rocky, roaring stream, some freak of memory suggested the singularly spirited old hymn : " On Jordan's stormy banks I stand." A thousand voices joined, and hill, and wood, and rock echoed and reëchoed the exalted strain.

The Cheat River, an exceedingly crooked and rapid stream, crossing the road repeatedly, and always difficult of passage, delayed the enemy. At the first ford, Captain Benham discovered the baggage-train at rest. He proposed an attack as soon as Barnett's artillery and Dumont's regiment should have come up; but the thoughtless firing of a musket gave warning, and set the train in motion. At the second ford, the Confederates were found to have left a few skirmishers. The advance opened a brisk fire, and cleared the adjacent wood. At the third ford, Carrick's, the rear of the wagon-train was standing. " Don't shoot," cried the teamsters, " we're going to surrender!"

The river at this point runs between a precipitous bluff of some fifty to eighty feet on the right, and low meadows on the left. The road on the left passes between the meadow-ground and the river, parallel to the river. The Confederates were strongly posted on the high bank, and hidden from view by a rail-fence and a tangled thicket of laurel.

As the Fourteenth Ohio advanced, a blaze of fire lighted up the bank and revealed the ambuscade. The Fourteenth halted, and, without a change of position, returned the fire. Barnett's artillery and the Ninth Indiana hastened to its support. The latter, being on the left, was obliged to fire obliquely, although the men crowded together, and next to the Fourteenth were thirty deep. The firing on both sides was rapid and fierce. Garnett's men aimed too high, and did little execution. Colonel Dumont, approaching through the meadow, (he had avoided the road on account of the mud,) heard the firing and ordered his men to advance on the run. He was met by a command from Captain Benham to cross the river three hundred yards above the ford, climb the hill,

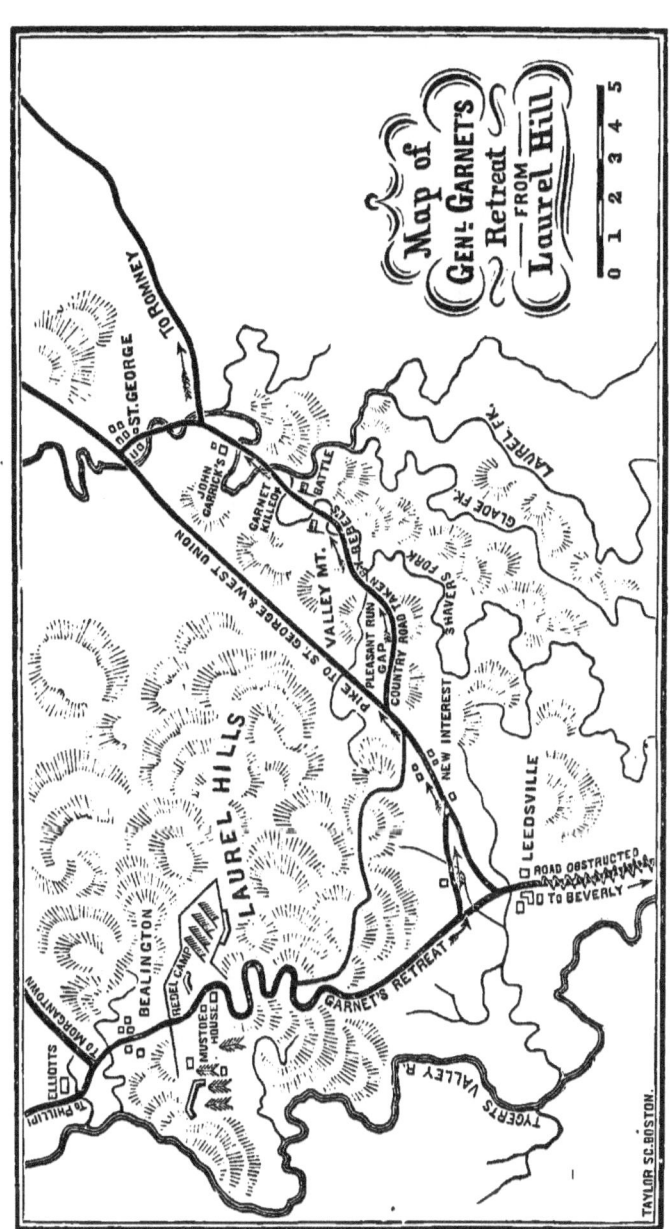

and attack the enemy in the rear. Without stopping, Colonel Dumont dashed straight through the river, dismounted, and climbed the hill by the aid of bushes and ledges of rock, which it was necessary to grasp at almost every step. Man by man, one company, two companies, almost three companies, followed, and reached the top, when an order was received to bring back the men, and to charge the enemy at the ford and at the guns. Unfortunately, Captain Benham had been told that the ascent of the bluff, except at the ford, was impracticable. His first order, had it not been countermanded, would certainly have resulted in the capture of a large portion, if not the main body of the enemy, without further pursuit or fighting.

Not a foot of ground lay between the river and the almost perpendicular bank. The river-bed was covered with loose rolling boulders. The current was rapid. The water in many places was waist-deep. Artillery was firing from each side. As might be expected under such circumstances, the passage from one point to the other was rapidly made. Guns and ammunition, held at arm's length, were kept dry.

Not until Dumont reached the road and appeared on his right, did the enemy turn to fly. A running fight ensued, and was continued to the fourth and last ford. Here again the enemy endeavored to rally. Through the tumult rose the clear, loud voice of General Garnett, cheering and urging his men to stand. In vain; and he stood with raised hand appealing to them, a single Georgian youth by his side, when a ball entered his back, and he fell. At the same moment fell his companion. They lay together, the General in his gorgeous Southern uniform, and the boy in his rustic butternut, when our advance approached, both dying. Colonel Dumont's pitying heart yearned towards the fallen Garnett, and he requested Gordon, who was always at the point of danger, to stay and guard the body. Gordon obeyed. He closed the eyes, tied up the chin, and straightened the stiffening limbs. No true and loyal man was ever more honorably cared for than this disloyal General. He fell strangely, in the rear of his flying army, and deserted by his own troops. Perhaps he was the victim of mortification and despair.

The sense of honor in the Southern gentleman is keener than the sense of right, and while it arms a man with daring courage, robs him of the nobler qualities of patience and fortitude. It impels him to rush on death rather than bear defeat.

Our soldiers buried the Georgian boy with gentle and respectful hands. The honor they showed him was no conventional thing.

In consideration of the exhausted condition of his troops, who had marched, almost entirely without food, twenty-seven miles, eighteen of which had been over a frightful mountain road, and in a pitiless rain, General Morris reluctantly ordered the pursuit to be abandoned. Colonel Milroy, however, like a man running down-hill, could not check himself short of two miles further. The closing sentence of an address which the General issued the next day, is: "Your cheerful endurance of the privations you have undergone, and are now undergoing, from the necessarily scanty supply of provisions, and the hardships of the march of yesterday over roads almost impassable, and through the storm of rain and battle, is — in the language of the immediate commander of the advance column, Captain Benham — most heroic, beyond all praise of mine, and such as your country only can fully appreciate and reward."

About forty wagons and teams were captured in the pursuit, also the colors of every regiment engaged. A Georgia banner was inscribed with the favorite Southern maxim, "Cotton is King." Eighteen or twenty were killed, and sixty-three prisoners were taken. Of Morris's army, two were killed and six wounded. The bluff on which the Rebel dead lay, was a ghastly sight, and blanched the cheek of the sturdiest.

The prisoners were not guarded, and were treated with cordial good-nature. Yet our men could not restrain their curiosity in regard to the desertion of Garnett, nor tire of asserting that they would stand by Morris to the last. Among the prisoners was a surgeon by the name of Carrington. He was captured under a stable, but, even in this trying situation, did not lose his self-possession. He introduced himself as a member of one of the first Virginia

## ABUNDANCE OF REBEL STORES.

families, happily unconscious that to the rude Hoosier the proud initials F. F. V. signified only fleet-footed Virginian. He also announced himself a descendant of Pocahontas, a fourth cousin of Mrs. General Scott, and an acquaintance of General McClellan. Not at all abashed by the mingled amusement and surprise in the faces of the gentlemen he addressed, he proceeded to accuse one of our surgeons of stealing a case of instruments, and threatened to report him to General McClellan. Later, he actually did report Federal officers to McClellan, and McClellan actually did arrest Federal officers on the word of this braggart.

According to General McClellan's report, the national loss on the two days, July 12th and 13th, was thirteen killed and about forty wounded. The loss of the Rebels was not far from two hundred killed and wounded, one thousand taken prisoners, all the baggage, and seven guns.

In the retreat the Rebel army was more fatigued and dispirited, but in every other respect had the advantage. The lowest number of the enemy engaged at Carrick's Ford was four thousand, while only eighteen hundred of the Union troops were up in time to take a part. Where Garnett was killed, but six hundred were engaged; they were members of the Seventh.

An article, in a heavy army-chest captured, excited some surprise. It was one of our bomb-shells. The prisoners said it fell, the day before the evacuation, about twenty feet from General Garnett's *marquee*, but failed to explode. The General considered his escape so narrow, that he extracted the fuse and preserved the shell as a memento.

The camp-equipage of the Rebels showed long preparation and lavish expenditure. The tents were the best Sibley; the blankets, cots, litters, of which they had hundreds, bandages, and surgeons' stores, were all of the finest quality; while the meagreness of the National tents, the coarseness of the blankets, the scanty supply of all kinds of utensils, the entire want of litters, and even of bandages, witnessed to the haste with which the National troops had been collected, and the unprepared state of the country. The contrast was significant and painful.

At St. George, to which place he proceeded next day, General Morris received orders to return to Laurel Hill. General Hill, who was at Grafton with fresh troops, was directed by the Major-General to intercept the enemy. Though without a leader, and dispirited and fatigued to the last degree, the Rebels eluded Hill and effected their escape.

The march of Morris's troops back to Garnett's old quarters was followed by a stay long enough to insure the destruction of the fortifications. The Eighth and Tenth, which had accompanied McClellan in his pursuit of Pegram to Beverly, assisted at the work. Then the veterans of the three months' campaign turned their faces homeward.

## CHAPTER VI.

### THE ELEVENTH.

THE Eleventh was the first regiment ready to march. It was trained by Lewis Wallace in the style of Napoleon's Zouaves, and it adopted the name which those fierce Algerines and their French successors have rendered a synonym of victory. Perhaps three fourths of the men were from Indianapolis and its vicinity. They were generally youths, high-spirited, generous, and intelligent, eager to win renown, and scornful of danger.

On the 8th of May they assembled in State House Square to receive two banners from the ladies of Terre Haute and Indianapolis. Tall, erect, in the bloom and vigor of young manhood, and glowing with enthusiasm, their appearance would have been striking without the aid of the showy foreign uniform. Colonel Wallace, who might be called the type of the regiment, received the banners, and turning to the soldiers, said, " Boys, will you ever desert these banners?" " Never! never!" shouted every man. Wallace then spoke of the disgrace cast upon Indiana by the alleged cowardice of our troops at Buena-Vista. " Let us adopt for our motto," he continued, " Remember Buena-Vista!" " We'll adopt it!" responded the regiment. " Then get down on your knees and swear that you will remember Buena-Vista, and that you will never desert your regimental colors!" The regiment kneeled, and with uplifted hand swore to stand by their flag and to remember Buena-Vista.

By a coincidence worthy of note, the same watchword was recommended to the South, through " The Memphis Appeal," one of its leading journals, in the following words: " If the great body of McClellan's forces be Hoosiers and Buckeyes, as reported, the number of our men need give the department little concern. *These fellows won't fight!* We have history for this. Remember Buena-Vista! One to four, our boys will drive them into the lakes." *

The 1st of May, the Zouaves were ordered to Evansville.

* The statement already made, that Jeff. Davis is responsible for the unfortunate reputation of the 2d Indiana, is based upon an assertion of General Lewis Wallace. The following note, written by himself, gives his reasons for the assertion: —

" According to history, General Taylor is responsible for the charge against our troops at Buena-Vista. As usual, however, his report was based on the statements, official and other, of subordinate officers. to whose conduct. suppressed and generally forgotten, my charge against Jeff. Davis is traceable.

"About two weeks after the battle, I had occasion to go to Saltillo. The controversy about the 2d Regiment was very warm. Being Hoosier-born, it was natural for me to take interest in it; and the conclusion I came to is reliable exactly in proportion to the reliability of the information it is founded upon.

" According to that information. the story of misconduct proceeded originally from General Jo. Lane and Jeff. Davis. A Court of Inquiry satisfied the former that he was mistaken, not in the fact that a large portion of the regiment retreated in disorder, but in his belief that it had no authority for retreating. The testimony is said to have developed (and it is now my recollection that such was the finding of the Court) that Colonel Bowles had ordered it to retreat in violation of tactical rules. Satisfied of this, Lane amended his official report. and requested General Taylor to do the same thing. General Taylor refused. instigated, as was understood by well-informed Indianians at that time, by Jeff. Davis.

" The reasons for this belief may be summed up: Davis claimed the victory for his regiment, the 1st Mississippi; even went so far as to claim that his was the only regiment that did not run that day: all his assumptions were vigorously disputed by officers from our State, who on their part asserted that the 1st Mississippi had turned its back along with the others, and that, in fact, the only regiment which had kept its front steadily to the enemy during the whole struggle. was the 8d Indiana, commanded by Colonel James H. Lane. Out of this dispute very naturally arose a red-hot quarrel.

" When the controversy among the officers from our State culminated in a Court of Inquiry, Davis sided, it was said, with Colonel Bowles. His regiment had formerly presented Colonel Bowles a Mississippi rifle, in token of appreciation of gallantry displayed, and the fact was urged as proof of his partiality. The particular accusation against the 2d Indiana, it must be borne in mind. was *cowardice;* and when in the dispute it was established that its Colonel had ordered the retreat. no doubt was entertained by our officers that General Taylor would officially relieve it from the charge. That he did not do so was at once attributed to Jeff. Davis, whose malignity was well known, while his near relation to General Taylor gave him influence to accomplish the end."

They left Indianapolis with delight at so soon getting into action. Their delight was premature, as the duties they were called upon to perform were no more active nor interesting than those of an ordinary police force. They examined vessels passing down the Ohio, to prevent the carrying of contraband goods, and they guarded Evansville, which was neither attacked nor threatened. The monotony of the camp was unendurable to men burning with the desire to do or die. When the heart is strung to the performance of a great deed, or to the offering of a great sacrifice, it is inexpressibly wearisome to be forced to count the moments, and to fill them with the stiff trifles of military life. The departure of three regiments from Camp Morton to the East added fuel to the fire of impatience.

June 5th, the Eleventh was ordered to Cumberland, in the department of General Patterson. Little time was occupied in preparation. From one o'clock on the morning of the 7th, at which time the train arrived, until daylight, when it departed, crowds of friends in the Union Depot at Indianapolis were uttering last words and last cautions. Danger, death, and grief, all the scenes and emotions of war, have become so familiar to our minds through the terrible battles of Virginia, Alabama, and Tennessee, that it requires some effort of the imagination to appreciate the anxiety and sorrow of the friends of our first Volunteers. Then the form of war was as unfamiliar as it is awful. It blackened the very sky. Many a true-hearted woman, who bade her son or her brother go, shut down her windows and drew close her blinds, that she might not see banners and blue coats, — might not hear the drum and fife.

The interest of the warm-hearted people of Ohio, and the ardor of the West Virginians, had not cooled; and the journey to Grafton was different in no particular from that of the regiments which had gone before. From Grafton to Cumberland the railroad passes through some of the most magnificent scenery in the United States. In winding down the slope of Laurel Hill, it springs over chasms of fearful breadth and depth, and at the base leaps boldly across the Cheat, a stream now dark with the sap of the laurel and spruce and pine forests in which it has its rise, soon, like many another American river, to be stained with brothers' blood. Almost lost in a savage pass, through which Snowy Creek alone sends a gleam, the rails again appear hanging on the rugged mountain-side, as if at the mercy of a gust of wind; then gliding down from mountain and pass, they cut a straight line through level and beautiful meadows.

Cumberland lies in a noble amphitheatre, with the laughing Potomac at its foot, and sunny slopes rising afar to forest-crowned peaks, all around. The fine old town has a history. Here the British, more than two hundred years ago, wrested an important fort from the French. Here the terror-stricken forces of Braddock found shelter after their disastrous defeat near Fort du Quesne. Here were Washington's head-quarters at one time, when he was in command of the Colonial troops. The stump of the pine, to which, according to tradition, he with his own hands nailed the Stars and Stripes, still stands. Our soldiers were not sufficiently familiar with the history of our flag to observe the anachronism; and they cut many a splinter from the venerable relic, and sent it home as a memento of the past and a token of the present.

The Eleventh was scarcely encamped, before Colonel Wallace had an expedition planned. Romney, a town among the mountains, on the west branch of the Potomac, in Virginia, formed the head-quarters of several hundred Rebel troops. These he determined to disperse. On the morning of June 12th, he went by railway, with about five hundred men, twenty miles, to New Creek Station. From this point it was necessary to proceed on foot over a rugged mountain-road, which afforded rare facilities to an enemy. About four miles from Romney the scouts captured a well-known Secession officer. To men who had been walking twelve hours, the sight of an important prisoner was agreeable. A little more than a mile from Romney they were fired upon by the enemy's advance guard, which then galloped forward and informed the camp. The approach of danger fired the spirits of the Zouaves, and they increased their speed.

The enemy was drawn up on the bluff, on which the town is situated, with two guns planted to sweep the road. Colonel Wallace called the attention of his men to a large house, about seventy-five yards from the farther end of the bridge, between them and the town; then gave the order to advance. They dashed over the bridge, leaped down an embankment at the farther end, and, as had been expected, received some scattering shot from the house. They rushed to the house and surrounded it, but not in time to prevent the escape of the pickets through windows and doors and up the hill behind. They now rapidly, but in a scattering manner, avoiding the road, pushed up the bluff to the right, with the double purpose of escaping the guns and cutting off the retreat. But " the legs of the enemy, their only trusty weapon of defence," did not fail them now. When the hill was gained, the road beyond was darkened with fugitives, — soldiers and citizens, women and children.

The Zouaves seized a quantity of arms and ammunition, some horses and provisions, then turned and walked back over a road which to footsore and wearied men was doubly dangerous. This expedition occupied but forty-two hours, although forty-six of the eighty-seven miles comprised were performed on foot; the road was rough, and not without danger in the night. Two dead and one wounded Rebel were left on the field. There was no Union loss.

A few days later, the Rebels burned a bridge, six miles from camp, and established themselves in force at Piedmont, twenty-eight miles west, on the railroad. Colonel Wallace's small force was now in a dangerous situation. The only reinforcements he could expect on short notice were two or three hundred Pennsylvania miners, who signified their willingness in case of necessity. Colonel Wallace daily sent mounted pickets, thirteen in all, to different posts along the several approaches to Cumberland. June 26th, the whole thirteen — D. B. Hay, E. Baker, E. Burkett, J. Hollenback, T. Grover, J. Hollowell, T. Brazier, G. Mulbarger, L. Farley, F. Harrison, H. Dunlap, R. M. Dunlap, and E. P. Thomas — were directed to proceed to Frankfort, a town midway between Romney and Cumberland.

In the evening of the same day, as the regiment was drilling on the hill-side, Harry Dunlap, his horse foaming and panting, was seen hastening toward Colonel Wallace. The word flashed along the line, surmise taken as fact: "All our scouts are prisoners or killed!" Anxiety was not allayed when Colonel Wallace, after rapidly giving some orders to an officer who stood near, called to Dunlap, as he turned: "Get off that horse. There is a horse," — pointing to a fine animal a citizen was riding up the hill, — " take him."

The stranger, seeming to comprehend the necessity for the singular order, quietly dismounted. Dunlap instantly sprang on the fresh horse, and away he flew. Fifty men, under Major Robinson, followed. Soon a covered express-wagon, surrounded by a large crowd of citizens, approached. Corporal Hay, the leader of the scouts, pale and bloody, lay within. The wagon stopped before the hospital-tent. The wounded man refused assistance, although he moved with difficulty. He had one sword- and three bullet-wounds, and had come ten or twelve miles since receiving them. Nevertheless he was able to give a spirited history of a great part of the day's adventures to Colonel Wallace.

The scouts went within a quarter of a mile of Frankfort, to a point from which they obtained a view of the village. To their surprise, they saw large numbers of both infantry and cavalry in the streets. A short reconnoissance was sufficient. They turned their horses' heads in the direction of Cumberland, and having come over the broad and direct road, they now, the better to scour the district, took a different route, which happened to be narrow, winding, and hilly. At a cabin-door they asked a woman, who stood watching them, with an interested and alarmed countenance, if any of the enemy were near. "Yes," she answered, "I counted forty-one, not five minutes ago, trotting along this very road." "Boys, shall we fight, or turn back?" asked the corporal, fight gleaming in his own eyes. "Fight!" responded all, and on they plunged. A man at the side of the road stopped them. "Rebels just ahead!" he said. "How far?" "Not fifty yards; around that bend."

The hour had come for which they had volunteered; the hour of revenge for Buena-Vista, and of glory. They reached the bend. Before them, trotting along leisurely, was a small body of cavalry. Clatter, clatter on the hill-side! The Rebels turned. Deceived by the bend, or by the furious onset of the approaching party, they fancied a hundred men in pursuit. One glance sufficed. "Neck or nought!" The horses caught the fear or the spirit, and neither whip nor spur they needed as they dashed on. The Zouaves did not even rein up to fire, but fired as they galloped. Suddenly the flying party came upon a deep gully. Several of their horses fell. There was no escape. The pursuers were at their heels. A desperate hand-to-hand fight ensued. Farley and a noted Texan ranger, a man of immense size, rolled down the bank, locked in each other's arms. The Texan cried for mercy. Farley loosed his hold, and sprang up. The Texan caught him by the legs and pulled him down again. Again there was a deadly struggle. Now one, and now the other, had his gripe on the throat of his foe. Both could never rise. Farley's hand failed. His limbs relaxed. One more blow, and the ranger would shake the dead man's hold from his massive body. Just then a bullet. The ranger released his clutch, and Farley staggered to his feet. Harrison had beaten off an assailant, when his eye fell on the struggling form of Farley, and he sent the ball which saved his comrade's life. Eight Rebels fell at this point. The remainder of the party fled on up the mountain. The scouts turned back into the road, and were engaged in binding up the wounds of Hay, when they saw the enemy returning, and in a force not less than seventy-five. One of the Dunlaps had gone for a wagon for Hay, and the scouts were now but eleven. Hay was placed on a horse and had sufficient strength to keep his seat, and to escape to the woods.

The corporal could tell no more. What had become of his comrades, he could not say. They came in, however, during the night, except two, Thomas and Hollenback, and finished the tale.

While Hay was making his escape into the woods, the remaining scouts abandoned their horses and waded to an island in the mouth of Patterson's Creek, which here flows into the Potomac. They could not have found a better position, but the odds were fearful. Eleven men on the low, defenceless island, more than seventy on the shore. Not a bullet must fail. Not a bullet did fail. With steady eye and steady hand, the scouts aimed at every man who entered the water; and Patterson's Creek was certain death to him who was so bold as to leave the shore. But the contest was too unequal to be kept up long. The water was crossed, the island gained, and yet not won. Foot by foot, inch by inch, it was disputed in blood. It is a fearful sight, men fighting for their lives! Now teeth were set, and fists were clenched. There was firing, and stabbing, and wrestling, and swearing, and praying. There was even pity in the wild fury of this combat. "I hate to kill you, but I must," muttered a Rebel, leaning over a Zouave, with bowie-knife upraised to give the fatal blow. A ball entered the divided heart, and the lifted hand sank powerless.

Twilight came, and under its friendly cover the scouts crept through the bushes, waded the stream, and hid in the woods; all but Hollenback. He lay helpless and bleeding on the island.

The next day Hollenback's lifeless body, shockingly pierced and mutilated, was found. His appearance excited suspicion; and the woman at whose house he was found asserted that he had been murdered. He was buried with the honors of war in the old cemetery of Cumberland, on the shore of that river whose melancholy fame was just beginning.

Hollenback was dead, murdered; and no man knew what had befallen Thomas. He had been seen to fall, but the island, the road, and the woods around had been searched in vain. Perhaps he lay in some dark gorge, perhaps in the river. Perhaps the Rebels had dragged him, wounded, into imprisonment. A heavy gloom rested on the camp.

As the evening sun was sinking behind the mountains, a cry ran from lip to lip, and swelled into a glad shout of "Thomas! Thomas!" On the brow of the hill the figure of a man was thrown in strong relief against the sky. It was the lost soldier. The regiment rushed towards him, and "every man felt as if his own brother had risen from the dead!" Thomas had been knocked down by a grazing shot over the eye. Scarcely had he fallen, when a hand was on his throat.

A shot from Grover delivered him from this second danger. He crept into a thicket and remained quiet until he could, unobserved, get to the hills.

The number of the enemy killed in this encounter was surprising. The woman at whose house Hollenback was found, said twenty-three were laid out on her porch. Neighbors confirmed her statement.

Certainly it was a most remarkable skirmish, whether we consider the number of the enemy slain, or the physical strength and skill, the steadiness of hand and eye, the readiness of thought, the coolness and resolution of the Zouaves, the fiery bravery with which they made the onset, and the patient bravery with which they withstood the assault. Kelley's Island is the least among battle-fields, yet its glory is not small. Here fell the first Indiana soldier.

The Eleventh received many attentions from the good people of Cumberland, but none which they appreciated more highly than a present of a garrison-flag, — with compliments to the bravery, kindness, and courtesy of Colonel Wallace's Zouaves — and a Fourth of July dinner. In honor of the Fourth, the camp was decorated with evergreens and flowers; and the exchange of positions, which imagination sometimes attempts in society, was proposed and effected with no confusion and much amusement. Officers carried guns and walked the rounds, while privates entertained company.

July 7th, the Eleventh received orders to join General Patterson at Martinsburg, and the same evening took up the line of march. The distance, ninety-seven miles, was accomplished in four days and a half. Forty thousand United States troops were now at Martinsburg; and the larger number, deceived by the easy conquest of West Virginia, anticipated a rapid march to Richmond. The superior officers, however, who knew the difficulty of obtaining supplies, and the danger of a sudden decrease of numbers arising from the expiration of the term of enlistment, looked forward to a battle with anxiety, if not with dread. General Patterson was ordered to prevent the arrival of General Johnston with reinforcements at Manassas. He visited the different brigades in person, represented that a battle was imminent, and urged them to stay a few days longer. Four of the nineteen regiments whose time was expiring, among them the Eleventh Indiana, came forward and announced their determination to remain, but fifteen could not be moved from their stubborn purpose to return to their homes. The fact that many men had left families unprovided for, and that their own clothing was worn out and could not be renewed, forms some slight alleviation to the disgrace of men who could march from the battle-field to the firing of the enemy's cannon.

With such a force as he could retain, and it was not small, Patterson approached Winchester, where Johnston was fortified,— approached, and stopped, and lay on his arms, while all night long the puffing of locomotives announced the departure of Rebel troops toward Manassas. He went to Charlestown, then back to Bunker Hill, and farther back to Harper's Ferry. He was not idle. In one or two warm skirmishes his advance was successful; and if marching and countermarching could have saved the battle of Manassas, then would Patterson have done his duty and won great renown. He was too far off to engage in the disastrous conflict which opened and closed on the 21st of July. Thus it happened that Indiana, in her grief for the national defeat, was spared the additional pang of recognizing her own sons among the sufferers in that strange panic which, for the hour, unmanned the noble and the brave.

The last week in July witnessed the return of the six regiments from the mountains of Virginia and the meadows of Maryland. They were engaged in no great battle in the three months' campaign; they did not suffer with heat nor with cold; they had no experience of malarious swamps and rivers, of thirsty sands, or of Southern prisons; and whatever hardships they endured were made light by the prospect of a speedy termination. The veterans, who have tramped from one end of the Republic to the other, and back again; who have besieged cities, blockaded islands, and bombarded fortresses; who have swept backward and forward, like a surging sea, upon a battle-field, not one hour, nor four, but all day and all night; may smile at the three-months' campaign, and talk of summer soldiers. But it should not be forgotten that these six regiments were among the pioneers of the war. They first sprang to arms, they first shouted the battle-cry of freedom, they first stood the shock of battle, they baptized the now truly sacred soil of Virginia with Indiana blood; and it is their dead who lead the stately but sad procession of Indiana's heroes.

The laurels won in the West Virginia campaign were not divided. The name of Morris does not occur in McClellan's reports. The nation, rejoiced in its hour of need to find a great man, did not criticise nor doubt, but confidingly placed the laurel wreath upon the offered head. Morris, who, in spite of the restraint laid upon him by his slow and strategetical superior, had shown himself quick, skilful, and prudent, and had won the greater part of the success unaided, made no attempt to gain public attention. He quietly withdrew to the duties of civil life. His indignant friends obtained for him at length from the seemingly unwilling Government the position of major-general, but could not induce its acceptance. As for the privates who were engaged in the three-months' campaign, hundreds of them, brave, intelligent, patient men, are still in the war, and are still privates.

## CHAPTER VII.

RESPONSE TO THE SECOND CALL OF THE PRESIDENT. — TROOPS STATIONED IN WEST VIRGINIA.

AFTER the organization of the six regiments of three-months' men, twenty-nine companies remained in Camp Morton, and sixty-eight in different parts of the State, in readiness, and begging for acceptance. Governor Morton, convinced that the President would call for additional forces, and that the State legislature, then in session, would provide by law for the organization of troops for the defence of the State, issued orders for five regiments of twelve-months' Volunteers. Camps of rendezvous were established in the following places: — Twelfth: Camp Morton, Indianapolis; Thirteenth: Camp Sullivan, Indianapolis; Fourteenth: Camp Vigo, Terre Haute; Fifteenth: Camp Tippecanoe, Lafayette; Sixteenth: Camp Wayne, Richmond.

The State legislature did more than accede to the proposition of Governor Morton. It provided for the employment of six regiments, and declared that they should be subject to the order of the Governor of the State to fill any requisition made for troops on Indiana by the President of the United States.

For the Seventeenth a camp of rendezvous was established at Camp Morton. Colonel Joseph J. Reynolds was appointed brigadier-general. General Reynolds is a citizen of Lafayette. He received his education at West Point. His name appears attached to the "Army Register of 1840," in conformity with a regulation requiring the names of five of the most distinguished cadets to be reported for this purpose at each annual examination. The legislature also made a law for the organization of the militia, and divided the militia into two classes — sedentary, and active. The sedentary militia comprised all persons liable to bear arms under the State constitution, except those enrolled in the active militia. The active militia, called also the home legion, consisted of all such citizens between the ages of eighteen and forty-five as should enroll themselves and take the oath of allegiance to the United States and the State of Indiana. The State furnished these persons with arms, equipments, and ammunition, and paid the expenses of drills. When called into active service, they were to receive the same pay as corresponding grades in the United States Army. They were to provide themselves with uniforms similar to that of the United States troops, and on being taken into the service of the General Government, were to receive compensation for the cost of their uniform.

On the 3d of May the President issued a proclamation, calling for Volunteer forces to serve three years or during the war. Four regiments were assigned to Indiana, accompanied by an earnest injunction to the Governor to call for no more; or if more were already called for, to reduce the number by discharge.

The second call of the President, and also the first, were no doubt limited by the want of arms; as, while Southern traitors were occupying positions in the United States Government, the armories in the Northern States had been almost stripped, and the contents sent South. On the 19th of April, fifteen thousand muskets in Harper's Ferry Armory had been destroyed, to prevent their falling into the hands of the Confederates; and the Springfield Armory, the only other dependence, was capable of producing only about twenty-five thousand muskets annually. Much time must necessarily elapse before arms could be brought from Europe. In addition to the want of arms, the President and his Council were greatly embarrassed by the continued discovery of traitors in high places, and by the state of the treasury, which was purposely reduced to bankruptcy by the preceding administration.

In pursuance of the orders from the War Department, the Thirteenth, Fourteenth, Fifteenth, and Seventeenth regiments were transferred to the United States service in an incomplete state. Governor Morton's policy of getting Indiana's quota for three years accepted before any attempt was made to re-organize the three-months' men, prevented the confusion that prevailed among the Volunteers of one of the neighboring States, the Governor of which commenced to form the three-years' regiments from the three-months' troops; and had also the effect of giving to Indiana six more regiments than would otherwise have been allotted to the State. The Twelfth and Sixteenth embraced all who declined to enter the United States service for three years.

Before the close of the three months, the Thirteenth was already in the field and actively engaged. The colonel of this regiment, Jeremiah Sullivan, was a young man, little more than thirty years old, but had served some time in the navy, and learned there the importance and value of discipline, — a lesson now to be put in practice to the advantage of himself and others. He arrived in Indianapolis from Madison, and reported to Governor Morton, with a company of one hundred and two men, the Thursday after the fall of Sumter. He was appointed commandant of a post, and engaged in disciplining Volunteers, until, on the 4th of July, he left Indianapolis as Colonel of the Thirteenth. Having arrived at Buckhannon on the 8th, and the next day reached McClellan's camp, twelve miles east, the regiment was in time to join in Rosecrans's morning-walk over the rocks of Rich Mountain. In the engagement with Colonel Pegram's rear, the Thirteenth bore the hottest of the enemy's fire, and suffered loss in proportion. Seven men were killed on this their first battle-field, and just seven days after their hopeful farewell to home. They were buried with tenderness and care. Their graves were covered with green sod, and marked with slabs inscribed with name and age. A simple and transitory tribute, — but their memory will ever be kept green.

The Fourteenth and Fifteenth regiments followed in the wake of the Thirteenth as far as McClellan's camp. These two regiments were made up respectively of Volunteers from the western, southwestern, and northern portions of the State. The colonel of the Fourteenth was Nathan Kimball, a graduate of Asbury University, and a physician in Loogootee. He was a captain in the Second Indiana regiment in the Mexican War, and distinguished himself in the battle of Buena-Vista by the skill with which, during the retreat, he brought off his men in company form, and the coolness and bravery with which he conducted them back to the battlefield, and fought with them during the day. When Colonel Bowles, who had given the disgraceful order to retreat, made his appearance at dress-parade after the court martial, the spirited captain refused to be inspected by him, and marched his men off the parade-ground. He was court-martialled for this offence, but his sword was soon returned to him.

The colonel of the Fifteenth was George D. Wagner, from Pine Village, a man of energy and nerve, who with few early advantages had made his way to a prominent place in the State Senate, and was President of the State Board of Agriculture.

During the 12th of July, all McClellan's by no means insignificant army stood ready for battle, awaiting the concerted signal, — the sound of firing from the rear of Pegram's camp. They waited in vain, and moved only when a messenger from Rosecrans brought information of the defeat and flight of the enemy. General McClellan then took up the line of march to Beverly, which place he made his head-quarters until called to a wider field. About the same time Rosecrans went towards the Kanawha, which the Rebel General Wise was threatening, and which was important as commanding the road to Cumberland Gap and to loyal East Tennessee.

The Fourteenth and Fifteenth were left almost alone guarding the Staunton turnpike from Beverly to Cheat Mountain Pass, fifteen miles east. In a few days they received a reinforcement of a company of Rangers, and a day later welcomed their new General.

General Reynolds had no staff and no body-guard. A member of General Morris's staff, Dr. Fletcher, formerly fife-major of the Sixth, expressed his desire to remain, and was at once transferred to the new General's staff, which he might be said to form, as for a while there was no other member.

The company of cavalry known as the Bracken Rangers offered itself to the General Government at the beginning of the war, under the President's call for Volunteers; and also to the State of Indiana, under an act of the legislature, passed at the extra session, held in the spring.

The policy of the General Government was not then to raise any but infantry regiments; and the State authorities declined to organize a force as provided by the act of the legislature. In the early part of June, instructions came from the War Department to have two companies of cavalry immediately organized and prepared for the field. On the receipt of these orders, Captain Bracken recruited his company, and went into Camp Murphy. Such was the enthusiasm in the formation of this company, that men too late to find a vacancy offered from ten to two hundred dollars for the situation of private.

July 19th, the company left Indianapolis. The citizens of Ohio were not yet tired of cheering, and the passage through that State was, as usual, like a triumphal procession. Although it was midnight when the train reached Dayton, thousands stood ready with a joyful greeting and more substantial evidences of consideration. At Webster, between fifty and sixty prisoners, taken at various places, were put under their charge and conducted by them to Beverly. While on the route an incident occurred showing the dangers to which travellers and trains are frequently exposed. In a narrow part of the road they met a train of wagons, and the horses attached to a wagon containing fifteen prisoners became unmanageable and plunged off the road, upsetting and dragging another wagon down the bluff. Tumbling and rolling, horses and drivers, prisoners and wagons, fell twenty feet together, without breaking a bone.

On their arrival at Beverly, the prisoners took an oath not to bear arms against the United States Government, and were released. Many of them immediately left for Staunton, some not without returning thanks for the kind treatment they had received.

The battles of Laurel Hill, Rich Mountain, and Carrick's Ford had driven the Rebels out of Western Virginia, and beyond the Cheat Mountain Range. The army of General Reynolds, being only an army of occupation, was divided into three camps, forming an almost equilateral triangle, with a mountain bridle-path forming the base line between the Elk Water and the Summit. The Staunton turnpike finds its way through Cheat Pass; and a branch-road, connecting Huntersville on the east with Huttonville, a village of some half-dozen houses situated directly in the pass on the west, runs a few miles to the south through Elk Water Pass.

General Reynolds established his head-quarters in the field, near Huttonville, and retained at this point the Thirteenth, and nearly half the Bracken Rangers. A small detachment of the latter was sent under Lieutenant Bassett to Elk Water, with the Fifteenth. Colonel Kimball, with the Fourteenth, already had possession of the Summit. Captain Bracken, with the remainder of his company, was also sent to the Summit. The Third Ohio, and batteries, consisting in all of about fourteen guns, were about equally divided among the camps. The whole force consisted of a little more than four thousand. The Summit and Elk Water, by the wagon-road, were eighteen miles apart; Huttonville, between them, was nearer the latter.

The Bracken Rangers were not again together on duty until the following February. Being the only company of mounted men attached to the brigade during most of this time, their duty as scouts, videttes, guards, and messengers was constant, laborious, and dangerous. No expedition or reconnoissance went out from any of the camps without being accompanied by a detachment of Bracken's cavalry, generally under command of a commissioned officer. The character of the country through which they were operating made it impossible to move off the travelled road, and rendered scouting on horseback extremely dangerous. At night, if not on duty, standing picket with horse in hand or mounted, they slept in their blankets, on pine or other boughs cut for the purpose. Such was their mode of life, and such it still is.

## CHAPTER VIII.

### GUARDING THE MOUNTAIN PASSES.

GENERAL REYNOLDS was fully aware of the responsibility of his position, as warden of West Virginia, and he immediately fell to work at the intrenchments. Both privates and officers lustily plied spade and axe until this trinity of strongholds seemed invulnerable to any but an immensely superior force. The fortifications on the Summit were built where the road makes an abrupt descent on both sides, having no level land on top. The tall white pines, which here grow very close together, were cut down for several acres, — the branches partially lopped and stripped, and the trees arranged around the camp, with the points out. Inside of this felled timber a strong wall of logs was built, and a deep ditch dug. Breastworks were thrown across the road on either side, in a line with the fortifications, and furnished with cannon, which on the east could sweep the approach more than a mile. In the rear of the fortifications there was no opening in the forest, except, at the distance of a mile or two, an old road, long abandoned and almost forgotten. The fortifications of Elk Water spanned the valley, which was about three hundred yards wide. They consisted of a deep and wide trench, and an embankment thrown up with a regular gradation, that the men might step up, shoot, and step back to load, in entire security. At the ends of the embankment were pieces on batteries ranging diagonally across the valley. The projector was Lieutenant-Colonel Owen.

On a fair day, a veil of blue mist hangs from two massive peaks at the head of the passes, spreads over the jagged outlines, north, east, and south, and lies along the rounded western hills which guard the valley of the Tygart. A small stream, showing in its sweet, transparent water the speckled mountain-trout and the white pebbles on its bottom, gives its name, the Elk, to the southern pass. A mile and a quarter east of the Summit, the dark cold Cheat dashes along its solitary and pine-bordered way to the Monongahela. Summer never tarries long in the mountain-valleys, and winter is always hovering over the mountain-tops. Even in August snow sometimes falls. In this cold, rugged, yet picturesque and beautiful region our soldiers were destined to remain many months. General Lee had collected Garnett's scattered forces immediately after their escape, and so added to them that in August he had an army of sixteen thousand. He fortified a position which nature had already made strong, on the Staunton road, as it ascends the Alleghanies; and sat down cautiously to watch his foes upon the mountains in his front. Lee is accredited by Pollard, the Southern historian, with a "pious horror of guerrillas." However this may be, our troops are confident that a regularly organized body of bushwhackers, numbering five hundred, was connected with his army, and that, though not acknowledged, they reported to somebody. Their leader was Jim Gum, a man whose appearance was suggestive of Lord Monboddo's theory of the origin of mankind. His matted, tangled locks, wandering eyes, and claw-like fingers,— the mournful expression which settled on his face when he was inactive,— were all like those of some wild, shy, vicious, mountain-creature.

The laurel, growing like a dense hedge close to the path and the roadside, afforded a hiding-place and safe retreat to the guerrilla. The teamster on the wagon which carried stores or mail to and from Beverly, Philippi, and Webster; the cavalry escort of an expedition sent out to buy forage; the picket at his distant post; the sentinel on duty, not out of sight of camp; fell victims to the sure aim of the stealthy murderer.

On the 9th of August, three cavalry men came dashing into the camp on the Summit, with the information, that, as they, with two other horsemen and one infantry man, were driving cattle along the Staunton road toward the Summit, they had been fired on from the bushes. Unable to turn out of the road with their horses, and unable even to see the enemy, they had fled, leaving three of their number, bleeding, on the ground. Exactly such an incident had occurred the day but one before, except that two men instead of three had fallen. In consequence, the blast which roused the camp explained itself. With no delay, cavalry and infantry followed Colonel Kimball, and traced the steps of the returned party. They had proceeded about four miles, when they met another party, bringing to camp two prisoners taken the day before, near the place of the attack. Colonel Kimball demanded of the prisoners — a sulky, almost idiotic-looking couple — the number and whereabouts of their gang. They refused to answer, — a right which all prisoners but bushwhackers have. Colonel Kimball wasted a few words in exhortations, a few more in threats; then, exasperated beyond endurance, raised his pistol and fired. In the words of one of the Rangers, " Then and there, in questioning them, the Colonel shot one of the prisoners, in order to make him talk. After which proceeding the prisoner talked, and was immediately cared for by a surgeon." The wound was not severe. This man was a murderer, and was captured as he lay in wait for assassination. As a partisan ranger or bushwhacker, he was an outlaw. Yet the generous and conscientious Kimball would surely not have fired on an unarmed prisoner, who had not yet received a trial, had he not been greatly exasperated and excited.

A mile or two farther, the three wounded men were found lying in the road. The guerrillas had appeared, after their comrades had left, and had fired again on one, Harry Cheyne, adding a second to his already mortal wound. They were taken up and carried carefully to camp. One died that night; another in two days; the third, Harry Cheyne, lay in the hospital on the mountain, until he was carried in a litter by his comrades to Beverly, where he lingered two months, an uncomplaining sufferer. His fellow-soldiers still speak of him affectionately and sorrowfully. They repeat that he had no hard feelings towards anybody but the man who shot him after he was down.

Only where the power of the United States Government was forcibly felt, that is, only where guerrillas were seized and punished without fail, did this sort of warfare become less prevalent.

General Lee is a strategist, disinclined to bold and dashing movements, averse to bloodshed, and fond of planning. He proposed to surround and entrap the Union troops; and to accomplish his purpose, divided his forces, sending fifteen hundred men, under Colonel Rust of Arkansas, along the road to the northern pass, while he himself crept toward Elk Water. While the former should keep the Summit engaged, the latter was to reach the rear and force the three camps, one after the other, to surrender.

As the opposing forces were daily brought nearer, reconnoitring parties frequently, and at many different points, came in contact. The immense forest, the ragged rocks, the winding course of the two roads and of the few by-paths, by obscuring an approach or an encampment, sometimes brought on unexpected engagements, and were conducive to unanticipated successes. One exhilarating day in August, a day inviting to adventure, Captain Hill of the Twenty-Fourth Ohio, which had lately been added to the little army, and Captain Thomson of the Fourteenth Indiana, left the Summit with about two hundred men, and advanced along the Staunton road two miles beyond our pickets. Here they spent the night. At dawn they renewed their march, although they were now almost within the enemy's outposts. Journeying along the still mountain road, they examined every opening and every ravine. Wherever on their return they might be cut off, they left a small force. At Hanging Rock, a dangerous point at the crossing of the Greenbrier, they left ten men, and pushed across the shallow stream with the remainder of their number, now about thirty. A drizzling rain and a heavy mist hid the mountains and obscured the valleys. They saw but a short distance before them, and came unexpectedly upon the Rebel pickets. Taking advantage of the mist, which concealed, if it did not magnify their number, they boldly attacked the pickets, drove them in, and captured three cavalry horses with equipments. They also captured a guard, quartered at a house on the roadside. Audaciously pressing onward, they turned a spur of the hill and came in full view of a thousand or more white tents, — infantry forming in line of march, and cavalry moving in the meadow below to intercept their retreat. One glance was sufficient. The thirty-two invaders of Rebel territory turned their back to the foe, and with the steady tread of men and the rapid tramp of horses behind them, reached and passed Hanging Rock, which the ten pickets were preparing to defend from a body of cavalry approaching by another route. Suspecting an ambush, the enemy at this point stopped the pursuit.

General Lee considered the attainment of the position he had planned by far the most difficult part of his undertaking; and when, after almost incredible exertions in the ascent of precipitous heights, and almost exhausting endurance of cold, he succeeded in planting himself on both sides of Elk Water, and Colonel Rust gained the crags of Cheat, he hoped to catch in his open hand the fruits of success. The brave spirits within the mountain fortifications were not prepared to succumb, the less so as they were not aware of the immense superiority in numbers of Lee's army. Since the middle of August, reinforcements, consisting of the Seventeenth Indiana and several Ohio regiments, had been received. General Reynolds now moved his head-quarters and all his available force to Elk Water, and prepared for a vigorous defence. The troops had every confidence in their General, their cause, and themselves, and saw the gathering and thickening dangers with delight.

During the second week in September, the mountains swarmed with Confederates. They were in front and in the rear; to the right and to the left. General Reynolds kept up constant skirmishing, kept men sleeping in the trenches, and the Rangers with their horses saddled and bridled.

September 8th, Sunday, Lieutenant-Colonel Owen, with two hundred and twenty-five infantry and four dragoons, to be used as messengers, was ordered by Colonel Wagner to proceed along the turnpike until he should meet the enemy, but to bring on no general engagement. The first night one half of the command slept on their arms, while the other half kept guard. They made no fires and preserved entire silence. Before daylight, they resumed their advance. They carefully examined both sides of the road; nevertheless they came so suddenly and so close upon a troop of Confederates, that a private of the Fifteenth, almost before he was aware, was engaged in a hand-to-hand scuffle. It was impossible to avoid an engagement, and Colonel Owen ordered his men to fire by sections, then to countermarch, re-form, and load in the rear. A brisk but brief action followed. A number of prisoners was taken. Not a man was lost. The prisoners represented their camp to consist of eight thousand men.

Monday, Colonel Wagner ordered Captain Templeton, of the Fifteenth, to advance with two companies eight miles along the Huntersville road, and hold a point four miles from the enemy's camp. Major Christopher of the Sixth·Ohio, with a hundred men, was placed in the rear, as a support. Wednesday morning, Captain Templeton's pickets were driven in. He sent for reinforcements. Colonel Wagner immediately sent the left wing of the Fifteenth, with Major Wood, and orders still to hold the position; but when in a short time a scout, who had been posted three miles to the east, reported a column of two thousand moving with the evident intention of cutting off Captain Templeton and Major Christopher, Colonel Wagner sent orders for the entire force to fall back instantly.

Wednesday night, Captain Coon, of the Fourteenth, was ordered to guard the bridle-path leading from Cheat Summit to Elk Water, a distance of seven miles. Taking with him sixty men, he left the sleeping camp on the Summit and proceeded down the mountain. Near midnight, finding the darkness so great as to render the woods impenetrable, the scouts bivouacked; but 'rousing at dawn, they set about their duty. During the same night General Lee had thrown into these same woods three regiments; and Colonel Rust, from his position in front, two regiments. These were now making their way to the right and rear of Cheat Mountain, and by this time were on every side of Captain Coon's company of scouts. Nothing however suggested danger, except the aspect of a farm-house, which, although known to be occupied the day before, was now closed and deserted. Captain Coon halted and sent two men forward. They returned and reported traces of six horses. A corporal, with four men, was immediately sent to reconnoitre more closely. The little squad crossed a narrow meadow, entered a wood, and commenced ascending a hill, before either sight or sound occurred to confirm suspicion. When half-way up the height, a salute of twenty or thirty muskets gave the required intelligence, brought the squad to a stand, and started Captain Coon forward. Several hundred muskets from the rocks above forced a retreat behind the steep bank of a small stream. From this shelter, Captain Coon and his company fired for a short time in safety, and with great effect; but by the threat of a flanking movement on the part of the enemy, they were driven back to several piles of logs. Here again there was a stand, and hot firing; again there was a threatened flanking movement, and again a retreat.

The great body of the Rebels, following the deserted road, had unobserved come between the Summit and the outposts, and concealed themselves within a few feet of the highway, waiting for sufficient light to enable them to make an attack. Not half a mile from camp they seized the supply-train, which left every morning at daylight and returned every afternoon with provisions. Shortly after, a single Ranger, going to his post, discovered the train without drivers and horses, and gave the alarm. Colonel Kimball, with twenty officers and two companies of the Fourteenth, Captains Williamson and Brooks, repaired to the spot to reconnoitre. Discovering the enemy, yet unconscious of his strength, he opened fire. He soon saw that he was opposed by a very large number; nevertheless he ordered his men to hold their ground, and had the pleasure of seeing the whole force of the enemy throw aside guns, clothing, and everything that impeded progress, and fly. Small scouting parties, at different points, engaged the enemy under the same misunderstanding as to numbers. The boldness of these little parties misled the Confederates. They supposed themselves discovered, and were the more easily intimidated.

Meantime Captain Higgins, of the Twenty-fourth Ohio, with ninety men, was out in search of Captain Coon. While pressing through the woods they received a volley from a hundred guns. Two or three volleys were exchanged; but Major Harrow, of the Fourteenth, coming up with two companies, and learning from prisoners the number in front, drew in the men and posted them, as advance guard, two miles nearer camp. Late in the day, Captain Coon and the larger portion of his men came in. They were torn and scratched by briers, and wet from wading numerous streams. They had been almost throttled by vines, had lost their hats and their shoes, and bore in their whole appearance evidence that they had barely escaped with their lives. Their comrades, now fully aware of the dangers they had endured and had escaped, greeted them with cheers and even tears of surprise and joy.

Lieutenant Junod, Company E, Fourteenth Indiana, at a picket station east of the Summit, with a force of thirty-five men, was attacked by five hundred. Junod was killed; as was also a private, George Winder. All the others escaped. One saved himself by throwing up his hands and falling as if lifeless.

In another warm engagement on the west, thirty were able to keep a position against several thousand. The same day, Thursday, early in the morning, General Reynolds despatched Britz and Pulver, two of the Bracken Rangers, and a telegraphic operator, with orders to Colonel Kimball. Not more than a mile from Elk Water, the messengers were warned by pickets of hidden danger along the bridle-path. Glimpses of horses, tied in thickets, confirmed report and suspicion; but Britz, who carried the despatches, was resolved to proceed. His comrades contended that to return would be in accordance with orders. Britz would hear no argument. "Go back, if you will," he said, "but the first obstacle shall not turn me from what I have undertaken. I'll go on if it cost me my life!" With that, he put spurs to his horse, and the spirited animal sprang up the broken path. Unwilling to desert their daring comrade, yet unwilling to proceed, the others followed more slowly. Suddenly the sound of rifles from behind the thickets! Rifles of the unseen foe! The bold Britz fell, shot through the head, and dead on the instant.

In turning, the telegrapher's horse stumbled and rolled down a steep declivity, crashing through bush and brier at least a hundred feet. Two days after, the man came into camp, unhurt.

Alarmed for the safety of Colonel Kimball, General Reynolds determined to force communication with the Summit, and he ordered the Second Virginia and the Third Ohio to cut their way by the path, and the Thirteenth to do the same by the road. The two commands started at three on Tuesday morning. They met with no opposition, and arrived at the Summit to find the camp rejoicing over the repulse of what was supposed to be mere reconnoitring parties.

On this same day, Captain Stough, of the Nineteenth, had a sharp engagement with a small number of horsemen, and carried from the field the body of an officer shot by Sergeant Lieber. That dead officer was a handsome man; but it was not his robust beauty and strength, lying in the helplessness of death, that hushed the group gathered around him in camp; it was his name—Washington. The dead man was John A. Washington, who made the burial-place of the Father of his Country a thing of merchandise. His treason was in accordance with his character, yet it was not in accordance with the laws of nature:—

> . . . . . . . . . . . . "For not at once
> Begets a house, a demigod, or monster;
> Only a line of evil or of noble
> Brings forth at last the wretch to curse, or him
> Who showers blessings." *

Men, rough in speech and thought, were conscious of the unfitness of his name. "What will George say to John when he goes up?" one asked of a comrade. "John will never go up," replied the other, gravely.

Saturday and Sunday very strong forces attempted flank

---

\* . . . . . . . . . . "Denn es erzeugt nicht gleich
Ein Haus den Halbgott noch das Ungeheuer;
Erst eine Reihe Böser oder Guter
Bringt endlich das Entsetzen, bringt die Freude
Der Welt hervor." *

*Goethe's Iphigenie auf Tauris.*

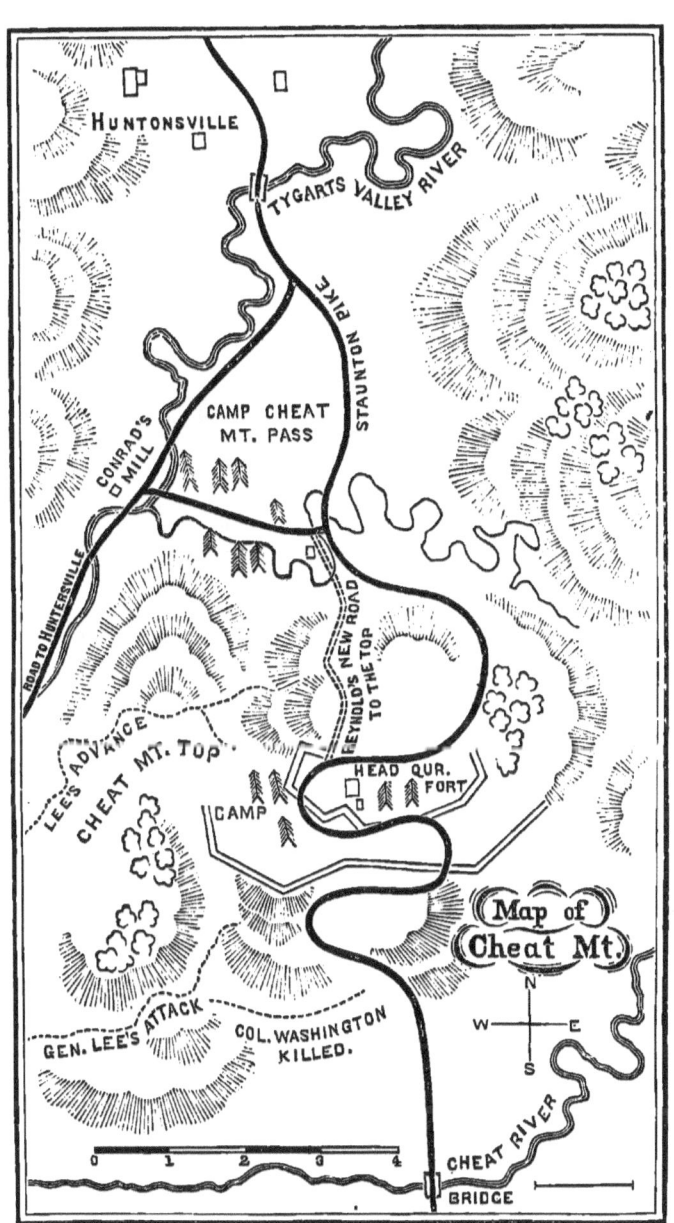

movements, but with no better success than on the preceding day. General Lee then gathered up his troops and retired, his rear completely routed on the retreat by the Thirteenth Indiana. The roads were left full of knapsacks, guns, and other proofs of the fatigue and alarm of the Confederates.

Seldom has a plan, so well laid as that of General Lee, so well and boldly carried out to the very last stage, failed so completely.

The mountains were climbed, the rear of the Union camps was gained; the camps were surrounded, and attacked repeatedly from every quarter. Lee's force was overwhelming in numbers; yet he could find no vulnerable point, and did not succeed in gaining a single salute from the batteries within the intrenchments. The communication between the camps was obstructed but one day. His failure was no discredit to him. It was due alone to the sleepless vigilance of General Reynolds and his officers, and the number and the daring of the scouting parties. Meeting armed men at every turn and at every step of advance, the Confederates imagined their number discovered, and their enemy in force; while the Federal troops in almost every instance supposed themselves engaging small scouting parties, and were rejoiced rather than elated at the series of victories.

Colonel Kimball had lost popularity since he had been among the mountains, from an unfortunate use of the word "machine," which, in insisting upon the necessity of discipline, he had applied to the soldier. To the Volunteer, fresh from the unrestrained and independent life of the American citizen, the term was suggestive only of the slavish life and character of the European soldier, and was, in consequence, inexpressibly distasteful. Probably no overt act on the part of one in authority, and certainly no word, could have been equally offensive. But in the hour of danger, Colonel Kimball showed himself so skilful in plan, so prompt in action, so watchful, so brave, and so regardless of his own comfort and safety, that the Volunteers, as generous in acknowledging merit as they were jealous of an invasion of personal dignity, not only forgave the obnoxious term, but gave to the Colonel the most hearty admiration and confidence.

Our loss in the engagements was singularly small — nine killed, two missing, and sixty prisoners. The killed from Indiana, besides those already mentioned, were two of the Fourteenth and two of the Fifteenth.

The ambulance, sent to bring in the remains of Junod and Winder, returned empty; the affectionate sharers of their danger insisting on carrying the dead in their arms.

The funeral ceremonies were performed the day of Lee's retreat. The scene was solemn and was rendered peculiarly impressive by the unusual circumstances and surroundings, — the tall dark firs and hoary rocks, the piercing wail of the trumpet and fife, the parting salute over the graves, and above all that strange feeling of nearness to the Unseen, which comes oftener and more thrillingly to the sojourner on the mountain-top than to the inhabitant of the plain.

Successful as was General Reynolds's repulse of Lee, he was convinced of the necessity of reinforcements, and earnestly represented his need to Governor Morton and to the War Department. Without waiting for orders from the Department, Governor Morton immediately sent to his aid the Seventh and Ninth Indiana, which were barely organized. When Milroy received orders to move, the regiment was not full, but he obtained permission to complete the number from the Twenty-eighth Indiana, which was recruiting at the same place. Orders from the War Department came the day after the regiments left.

During the latter part of September and the first of October, the light showers, common to all mountain regions, gave place to furious storms. Quiet brooks, which in summer wind their rippling way around the rocks, and gently wash the bared roots of pine and oak, now tore rocks and trees from their foothold or dashed over them, sweeping along every less firm obstacle. Summer breezes became roaring, howling, shrieking blasts. The motionless mist was swept away by a dull, driving army of clouds.

The night of September 27th was fearful. Rain fell in torrents. The blast through the narrow gorge of Elk Water was like the pealing of a gigantic trumpet. The trembling tents started from their foundations. The Elk rose, and dashed down a great part of the fortifications, and threatened to carry away blankets, clothing, and men.

None were so exposed in these autumn storms as the pickets at their distant and solitary posts. A little party of soldiers sometimes watched for days together in some untravelled bridle-path or on some ledge of rocks, where the stillness of day was not less than that of night, and was never broken except by the rattle of the creeping snake, the stealthy step of the mountain-fox, or the cry of some more savage animal. The squirrel and rabbit live in milder regions; birds also seek a warmer climate. There could be few severer tests of physical courage than the dreary beat of these distant sentinels. One night, a single Ranger was riding along the mountain, through a forest which added its shade to the darkness of a moonless and cloudy sky. Unable to see, and therefore unable to pick his way, he proceeded slowly, his horse's hoofs, now crushing a dead limb, now starting a loose stone, alone breaking the stillness. Suddenly a rustle, a gleam, the quick springing and trampling of feet! Almost before the thought of bushwhackers could form itself, a line of motionless figures stood before him. That creeping, icy terror, which in a moment of awful danger is not unknown to the stoutest heart, froze his blood. He waited the deadly click of the rifle. A minute, and no sound; another, still no sound. Then, to the equal amazement and relief of horseman and horse, the foe turned, and swiftly leaping back into the forest, revealed a body of startled deer.

The storms of September converted the turnpikes into long and deep stretches of mud; and wagons were three and even four days coming from Webster, fifty miles, whence all army stores and mail-matter were brought. Government horses suffered sadly, drivers, in their impatience, neglecting alike the dictates of humanity and honesty.

With the first week of October, the storms passed away; and the sun — shining over forests lighted up with the glorious hues of autumn, the dying leaf only the more brilliant from its proximity to the fadeless needle of the evergreen — revealed a magnificence double that of summer.

During the summer and the greater part of the fall, the

troops suffered for want of proper clothing. They had scarcely built their fortifications before they felt the necessity of a warmer dress, July though it was. General Reynolds sent a requisition for overcoats, but it received no attention. A second requisition met with no better success. He applied to Governor Morton, but it was long before even Governor Morton was able to elicit anything but despatches from neglectful officials. Agents asserted that clothing had been bought; clothiers, that it had been sold; railroad-men, that it had passed over the road. The information and reports seemed satisfactory and accurate. But no clothing reached the Cheat Mountains, and no railroad official could ever trace its route. Three messengers, sent on an exploring expedition, returned unsuccessful. A fourth, while burrowing in a warehouse on the Kanawha, to his surprise and delight, came upon several boxes of United States uniforms. They had been soaked in a freshet, and had lain until they had rotted, and were now useless. But the discovery added the impetus of hope to the search. More boxes were found. Yet thousands of suits were not discovered and not accounted for. Though there never has been an exposure of all the circumstances, it is certain that greedy men caused much suffering to our faithful and patient soldiers that summer and fall.

During the search and investigation, the Volunteers continued their acquaintance with mountain breezes and storms, their tatters flying like flags, their blue fingers showing the grip of ague, and their bare feet steadily pursuing the guard's rough round. Not until November was passing into December did rags yield to whole and comfortable garments. He who would rob our Government or our soldiers, is capable of any crime, and incapable of any virtue.

General Lee went to the Kanawha region, immediately after his unsuccessful attempt upon the Federal fortifications, and left General H. R. Jackson with a large force strongly intrenched ten or twelve miles southeast of Cheat Mountain Summit, on a series of natural terraces, which form the slope of one of the Alleghany Mountains, and which offer an extraordinarily advantageous position for defence. The valley at the base of this slope is almost oval in form, encircled by hills, and terminated at the northwest extremity by the Cheat Mountain, on the Summit of which had so long been Colonel Kimball's head-quarters. Its width varies from two miles to half a mile; its direct length, from the foot of one range to the foot of the other, is little more than six miles. At the base of the Cheat the road crosses a branch of the Greenbrier; at the foot of the Alleghany it crosses the Greenbrier. On the road at the river-crossing stood a tavern called the "Traveller's Repose," and at a little distance a mill. The fortifications began immediately behind these houses, the mill-race serving as a moat for parts of two sides, and extended into the forest which crowned the Summit and which stretched down to the water's edge, completely concealing a great part of the defences, especially on the left flank. Particulars in regard to the position and strength of this camp, called Camp Bartow, were unknown to General Reynolds, and, as the valley was held by Rebel pickets, their line extending to the very base of the Cheat, could be obtained only by a reconnoissance in force.

In consequence, he determined, in the latter part of September, to make an armed reconnoissance, and sent the Ninth and Fifteenth in advance from Elk Water to the Summit. The commencement of the expedition was not auspicious. Having been ordered not to encumber themselves with baggage, the men were without tents, and, during four days' detention on the bleak Summit, were exposed, entirely unsheltered, to fiercely inclement weather. Crouching amid rocks and brush, in water and mud, they endured a rain which poured down forty-eight hours without a moment's cessation. The cold was so bitter, and the want of sleep so exhausting, that some of those brave and patient men, uninured as they yet were to hardship, wept like children; and the officers, Milroy especially, full of affectionate concern and sympathy, often felt their own eyes blinded with tears during those terrible hours. A number sank under the exposure and were carried to the hospital. The suffering was not confined to the men, — several horses and mules died from the cold.

At midnight of October 2d, the movement towards Greenbrier began. The force consisted of about five thousand: three Ohio regiments, two batteries, and a part of a third; three cavalry companies, Bracken's Indiana, Greenfield's Pennsylvania, and Robinson's Ohio; and the Seventh, Ninth, Thirteenth, Fourteenth, Fifteenth, and Seventeenth Indiana. The four last-named regiments had been greatly reduced by exposure, hard service, and sickness. In September, when Lee made his onset, the few sick threw down their blankets, snatched up their guns, and ran from the hospitals to the ranks; but now about half the men, as they were roused at midnight, lay and listened to the heavy tread of the departing force with only a languid interest. The Ninth led the advance. The night was dark. The march was in silence, except when trees had to be chopped from the road. At daylight they arrived at the bridge over the north branch of the Greenbrier, about four miles from the Confederate Camp. A lively skirmish took place here between Confederate pickets and two companies of the advance. One of the Ninth was killed, and another slightly wounded. The pickets retreated rapidly; and the Ninth dashed after them, not stopping until ordered to halt, within two miles of the Rebel camp, for the artillery.

The front of Camp Bartow was hidden from view by a densely wooded hillock, which in its thickets now sheltered between six and eight hundred of the enemy. Colonel Kimball was ordered to clear a place on this knoll for Loomis's Battery, Colonel Milroy and Colonel Dumont to march along the river to the right, and be prepared to give assistance if needed. With a shout, the ragged Fourteenth rushed up the hill-side. A warm contest ensued. The Confederates fought with a spirit they had not before shown, and yielded the ground only as they were driven. The Ninth and Seventh pouring on their flank, they were forced to the left, their own right, and back to their fortifications.

Within about seven hundred yards of the intrenchments, the National troops halted, and throwing themselves on their faces, lay nearly an hour, while an artillery duel took place over them. It was a singular situation, at least for raw troops, — Loomis and Howe and Daum in their rear, Confederate cannon booming in their front, the mountains echoing the hollow roar of guns and multiplying the shrill shriek of shells. Yet in spite of novelty, tumult, and danger, some of the men were so weary, that they fell asleep.

During the hottest of the firing, rockets were observed to go up from the camp; and soon after reinforcements of perhaps five thousand were seen coming down the road behind the enemy. General Reynolds, who stood on a knoll in a line with the batteries, was able to observe the movements of both armies without a glass. He thought the Confederate force, before the arrival of the reinforcements, amounted to about five thousand; and he did not consider it prudent to continue the attack, especially as he had gained the information he desired. But some appearance on the part of the enemy of a movement on our left flank, and the urgent entreaty of the officers who surrounded him, induced General Reynolds to give orders for an attack on the enemy's right. For this purpose the troops supporting the batteries were hastily summoned; and the Rebel troops were met by the Seventh, Fourteenth, and Fifteenth Indiana, and the Twenty-fourth Ohio. The Seventh, a raw regiment, which had as yet scarcely heard the sound of cannon, was put in the van, and received a furious storm of balls. Some say it hesitated, others, authority as good, assert that it not only held its ground, but advanced. Certainly it did not run; and when, after a short but fierce contest, orders to retire were given, the Seventh, as well as the other regiments engaged, retreated in good order.

The desire to resume the attack was loudly and universally expressed, but the orders were peremptory, and the troops were obliged to turn their back to the enemy. They marched away slowly and sullenly, the Ninth bringing up the rear, and burning with indignation as cannon-balls and traitor cheers were hurled after them. They seized every pretext for lingering, in the hope of being pursued and forced into a decisive engagement. But the Confederates could not be enticed from their stronghold, and the Union troops reached Cheat Mountain Summit in safety and unmolested. They had marched twenty-four miles, and had been under fire four hours.

The National loss was nine killed, six of these were Indianians; thirty-two wounded, — an extremely small loss for so severe a combat. It is affecting to see in the list of the killed, after the name of J. Urner Price, a member of the Fourteenth, the simple remark, "He died a Christian as he had lived one."

The Confederates had three guns disabled, and lost, according to their own account, fifty men. General Reynolds, whose estimation of numbers is always very moderate, reckoned their loss over two hundred.

On the return the Seventh discovered, to its consternation, that its banner was missing. The color-bearer, called to account, was obliged to confess, that, when the troops supporting the batteries were ordered to throw themselves on the ground, he had put the banner, for safe-keeping, in a fence-corner, or against a tree, and having fallen asleep, had forgotten it when roused to join in the attack on the enemy's right. 

This ridiculous incident gave to the Seventh the title of Banner Regiment, — a title given in mockery, and received in some mortification, but fitting to be worn now in all honor by the men who fought at Port Republic. The battle of Greenbrier closed the campaign.

Milroy had been appointed Brigadier-General, September 3d; but a brigade was not assigned to him until the second week in October, when he was given the command of the brigade at Cheat Summit. He at once commenced an active system of daily scouting, particularly in the direction of Greenbrier, which place he supposed General Reynolds would attack again. Milroy's scouts several times passed around Greenbrier Camp, and had skirmishes with the Rebels on all sides of the fortifications. The enemy began to think their position unsafe, especially as Jackson, who had now withdrawn from the Cheat Mountain region, had greatly diminished their number; and they fell back nine miles, to a point on the Alleghanies, which they strongly fortified.

General Milroy, with a portion of his forces, followed them up the day after they fell back; he found a large amount of camp equipage about the deserted fortifications, with several pugnacious epistles addressed to him and his troops. He followed to the immediate vicinity of Alleghany Summit, where he captured a Georgia soldier, from whom he learned the situation and strength of the forces there.

General Milroy gave his personal attention to every duty, and frequently hastened a lingering job with the strength and skill of his own arm. On one occasion, thinking that his men were long in repairing a bridge, he got off his horse and went into the water up to his waist, to assist in arranging the logs. While he was at this work, a teamster came along and commenced cursing the men for their tardiness. The General looked up and said, "You look pretty stout; suppose you give us a lift." "See you damned first!" was the surly reply. "Look here," said the General, "if you give us any more of your abuse, I'll come up there and pummel your head with a stone." The teamster went on, and soon met with an acquaintance of whom he inquired, "Who is that gray-headed cuss back there at the bridge? He's mighty sassy." "Why!" exclaimed the acquaintance, "that's our Old Gray Eagle!" The teamster, who already had had some misgivings, returned to apologize.

Much time was spent in building substantial cabins. The sound of the axe and the saw, accompanied by joke and song, enlivened the forest, and gave promise of comfort to the coming winter. The last week in October the troops were inspected by Major Slemmer, of Fort Pickens' fame. He gave them high praise, not only for the cleanliness of their camps and clothes, and for the brightness of their arms, but for the superiority of their discipline. He ranked them among the best drilled in the service.

October 28th, the Thirteenth left camp on a reconnoitring expedition through the southern part of Randolph, and through Webster county. They took no baggage, carried their provisions, which consisted of four days' rations, on mules, and were prepared with axes to chop their way. They plunged, almost at once, into a pathless wilderness, through which they were five days journeying. They were frequently obliged to cut a passage through dense thickets; and once could find no place for their feet except in the bed of the Holly, which they traversed eight miles. They slept nightly on beds of moss, which were softer than the finest mattresses, but saturated with rain. The 1st of November, at noon, while they were at the foot of a steep mountain covered with trees and underbrush, a heavy volley was poured on them from above. Two companies immediately charged up the mountain, although no enemy was visible. They soon discovered the ambush, and drove the enemy back about three hundred yards. At this distance the Rebels rallied, and again seeking shelter, continued the fight for a very short time, when they fled. The Thirteenth, being already weary with a march of eighteen miles, encamped on the spot for the night. Beyond the Little Kanawha they discovered a block-house, evidently newly built. They approached with some caution, but found, to their surprise and delight, that the garrison, consisting of nearly a hundred, was loyal. The mountaineers of the region, who were faithful to the Government, had found it necessary to defend themselves from the Moccasin Rangers, a military company sworn to exterminate Union citizens, and had just finished the fort, in which they expected to find protection until they could call for and receive assistance. The spectacle of sturdy patriotism afforded by these honest mountaineers repaid the soldiers for many a weary mile; and the hearty sympathy and admiration they bestowed was not less grateful to the Virginians. They met and parted with the cordiality of brothers.

The Thirteenth took the Rebel mail, on the line of communication between two portions of the Rebel Army, a large quantity of Confederate money, and thirteen rancorous Secessionists, four of whom were bushwhacking at the time of their capture. The remaining seven belonged to the military company of which mention has already been made. The prisoners were preposterous specimens of humanity, savage and snaky, like Indians, — but stupid in countenance, drawling in speech, lathy in form, and dangling in movement. They evinced no distress, nor anxiety, nor curiosity, nor regret. They seemed passionless, yet they had shown themselves fearfully blood-thirsty.

The Thirteenth reached camp, hungry, haggard, and dilapidated, but well satisfied with having explored in nine days one hundred and eighty miles of the wildest region in West Virginia.

## BATTLE OF ALLEGHANY.

General Reynolds and the larger number of his troops were ordered to leave West Virginia about the first of December. General Milroy was put in command of Cheat Mountain district, embracing the posts of Beverly, Huttonville, Elk Water, and Cheat Mountain; and one regiment was assigned to each post. Being left to himself, with the Ninth Indiana, the Twenty-fifth and Thirty-second Ohio, Second Virginia, and Bracken's Cavalry, Milroy immediately commenced preparations to attack the Rebel works at Alleghany Summit. The Thirteenth Indiana, although under orders to leave, had not yet left Beverly on the 12th of December; and General Reynolds, who was also still at Beverly, sent up about three hundred of the Thirteenth, and one hundred of the Thirty-second Ohio. These, with the Ninth Indiana, (five hundred,) Twenty-fifth Ohio, (four hundred,) Second Virginia, (two hundred and fifty,) and about thirty of the Rangers, moved on the 12th toward the Confederate camp. At Greenbrier, the old Camp Bartow, about eleven o'clock at night, Milroy divided his forces, and sent Colonel Moody with the Ninth and the Second Virginia to make a *détour* to the right for the purpose of reaching the left flank of the Rebels, which commanded the Staunton turnpike. Milroy left Greenbrier about an hour after Colonel Moody, and going on the direct road, reached the vicinity of the Confederate works about daylight, a little later than the concerted time of attack.

He sent his detachment to the left up the hill. At the top they fell in with a strong picket-guard, which they endeavored to capture, to prevent discovery, as they were directed to remain in the woods until they heard firing from Moody, at the other side of the camp. A part of the pickets escaped and gave the alarm; and when Milroy's detachment emerged from the woods, it was met by the whole Confederate force, about two thousand strong. After a desperate engagement of about half an hour, the enemy was driven into his works, which consisted of huts, built so that they formed fortifications with a hollow square. Milroy's men charged gallantly in after them, and for a time held part of their works. They were forced back, but repulsed the Rebels with great loss to them every time they attempted to advance beyond their works. The fight was thus kept up until the Union troops had no more ammunition, and hearing nothing of Colonel Moody on the other side, became discouraged. General Milroy was reluctantly compelled to retire from the conflict. He carried with him his wounded, and thirty prisoners, and retired in good order.

Scarcely had Milroy reached the base of the hill, when Moody arrived at the top on the other side. He had been detained, first by the wretched nature of the roads, afterwards by obstructions of trees and brush. Near the camp the obstructions were so great, it was almost impossible to advance. The sound of cannon seemed to restore the exhausted strength of his men. They made their way over breastworks and through ditches until the very last line was reached. There they fought four hours with fiery and desperate energy, but neither the valor nor skill of so small a force could avail against the whole Confederate power massed at this point; and baffled, overcome, they were at last obliged to turn and retreat.

Could Colonel Moody have attacked simultaneously with Milroy, there is little doubt that the assault would have been a complete success. As it was, it was a melancholy, an utter failure.

Costly blood sprinkled that Rebel hill; and not the least precious was that of Joseph Gordon, a beautiful, brave youth, whose culture, talent, and lofty aspirations gave promise of a noble career. Shot in the forehead, he fell almost at the cabins of the enemy, and while his clear, young voice, calling to his comrades to "Come on!" was still ringing through the woods.

The number of National troops killed was twenty-four; wounded, one hundred and seven; missing, ten. The exact amount of the enemy's loss is not known.

## CHAPTER IX.

### THE BRACKEN RANGERS.

DURING the months of August and September Bracken's Rangers were employed night and day, — nearly all the time on half rations, seldom on full, frequently without any. Hay was furnished as it could be procured in the neighborhood; corn and oats from Webster by wagon, a distance of over fifty miles. Early in October they were sent to Beverly to rest and to pasture the horses. In November they were recalled, excepting a small number, and scattered about among the different posts. Those remaining in Beverly had the county jail — a large, comfortable, two-story brick building — assigned them as winter-quarters. They had charge of the prisoners captured, conveying them from time to time to Grafton, for transportation to prison at Columbus, Ohio. This duty was severe, as it was performed in midwinter, when the roads were almost impassable. A progress of a mile an hour was "on time." When from necessity the speed was increased to a mile and a half an hour, both prisoners and guard suffered and complained.

The efforts of the members of the company to be Rangers not only in name but in fact, fully succeeded. They were to be found wherever there was "forage and rations," and sometimes where there was neither. They made an unusual number of acquaintances. Even the Secesh girls, who had "cousins" in the Rebel Army, did not hesitate to give them a bright smile. This happy disposition to wander led to the discovery of the hiding-places of wild turkeys, geese, ducks, and such other animals as are accustomed to make sudden attacks on soldiers, biting them severely. Their quarters, New-Year's eve, were filled with these dangerous animals, the Rangers intending to guard them till high noon, when they would take ample satisfaction for all past sufferings. But the General had prepared a different feast. Daylight found them mounted, their horses' heads turned southward toward their old camping-ground at Huttonville.

An expedition had been planned against Huntersville, a rendezvous and depot of supplies for the Rebel Army and guerrillas. Detachments from the Second Virginia, Twenty-fifth Ohio, Bracken's Cavalry (under Lieutenant Delzell), in all six hundred men, under the command of Major Webster, of the Twenty-fifth Ohio, formed the expedition. They encamped that night at Big Spring, — so named from one of the large and beautiful springs common in these mountains. No one in that command will forget the darkness of that night, or the terrible wind which swept down the mountain gorges.

Taking a soldier's breakfast, the troops pushed on, not only success but their safety depending upon their reaching Huntersville before reinforcements could be sent there. The second night they encamped at the commencement of a blockade of the road made by Lee's army on its retreat from Elk Water the previous September. It was formed of felled trees, was a mile in extent, and in some places twenty feet high. It formed a complete defence, impassable even to a footman. Gathering pine boughs for beds, the troops clustered around the fires which lighted the gloomy aisles of the pine forest. The Rangers, as usual, faring better than their comrades, had saddles for pillows. Leaving the wagons the next morning, they scaled the mountain sides, the cavalry horses being led over untrodden paths. By ten o'clock they had reached the open road. At the bridge over Greenbrier River, the enemy was first discovered in strong works, prepared to dispute the passage; but the cavalry fording the river above the bridge, the enemy fled without firing a gun.

Major Webster pushed on to Huntersville, six miles distant, meeting with no resistance, until reaching the valley in which the town is situated. The Rebels, strongly posted, opened fire upon the advancing troops, who instantly formed into line and charged into town. The Rebels retreated. It was but the work of an hour to destroy the village and a large amount of army stores. Major Webster immediately started on his return. He reached camp the seventh day, without the loss of a man.

The Rangers resumed their usual occupation of scouting, guarding prisoners, and carrying messages, when Captain Bracken was ordered to proceed, *via* Buckhannon and Clarksburg, to Parkersburg. The place was reached about the first of February. Comfortable quarters and sufficient forage were for the first time furnished the horses.

## CHAPTER X.

### THE TWO SCOUTS. BY W. B. F.

ON the morning of the 26th of July, General Reynolds and staff left the little town of Webster, and took up the line of march southward along the Staunton 'pike. The day was hot and dusty. A few straggling soldiers were found along the road,—and occasionally an army-wagon came lumbering down the hills. One day's rations in our haversacks prevented our stopping by the way for dinner. So we rode steadily onward till we came to Philippi, where Clark and I called upon some of our old acquaintances, who were much surprised to see us, as they had bidden us good-bye only a few days before, expecting never to see us again. We told them that we had made up our minds to serve under the new General during the war. Philippi had resumed its business-looks, and we passed through, going on some six miles, and reached our camp on the farm of Mr. Thompson, — or the Half-way House, as it is called, being half-way between Philippi and Bealington.

Early in the morning, as we were striking tents, Old Thompson came down and presented a bill of ten dollars for camping on his farm. General Reynolds asked if he was a Union man. He said he was; but nevertheless demanded damages for our lodgings; and received a damning at the hands of Captain Keyes of the First Pennsylvania Cavalry who was acting as escort to the General.

We resumed our march, stopping a few moments at Elliott's, and at the old Rebel camp at Laurel Hill, where we took in a stranger, who proved to be Larz Anderson, brother of Major Anderson, (of Fort Sumter,) who was going to Beverly to see his sons, who were in the Sixth Ohio. We had quite a pleasant ride over a good road, through a picturesque country, not thickly inhabited, and at four P. M. arrived at Beverly, where we made a halt of an hour, while General Reynolds gave some orders. Here we found the Sixth Ohio and First Virginia regiments, and Bracken's Indiana Cavalry.

About five we started on southward, crossing and recrossing Tygart's Valley River, which grows smaller continually and more crooked, and more cramped in among the mountains. The scenery was grand and imposing. The narrow valley was locked in by mountain barriers, which seemed piled up, roll upon roll, away into the blue mists of the summer evening. We advanced along narrow passes, turned and crossed the river repeatedly, — and went on, — locked in by steeper, more wild and wrangled heaps of land and rock and woods: such was the journey on to Huttonsville.

Huttonsville consists of a bridge, a barn, storehouse, mansion, and stable, — all but the bridge belonging to Mr. Hutton. Crossing the river, and proceeding some three miles, we come to what seems the end of the valley, where we see in the twilight the flickering of a thousand camp-fires. We pass the sentinel, cross Tygart's Valley River once more, and find ourselves in camp at Cheat Mountain Pass. We ride down the clean wide streets, and halt before the tent of Colonel Sullivan, Thirteenth Indiana Volunteers, where we dismount from our weary horses, and partake of the Colonel's coffee; and after listening to the band which serenade our General, we roll ourselves up in our blankets, and are soon dreaming as only a tired soldier can dream.

July 28th, we were up early, trying to draw rations for our men; but General Sleigh, who was then in command, would not sign a requisition. In fact, he would n't "attend to any d—d business" before nine in the morning. I did not feel like waiting for General Sleigh that long. I knew General Reynolds would take command that day, so I informed him what my opinion was of a young General who would lie there in his tent and keep fifty men hungry. He swore he would have that fool arrested, but did n't come out of his tent. I went to a wagon and took what provisions were needed, and at last we had our breakfast. In looking around the camp, I found several Indiana boys, all looking well and full of life.

Camp Cheat Mountain Pass seemed shut in from all the world, for the mountains, with their tops lost in the cloudy mist, stand up on every side.

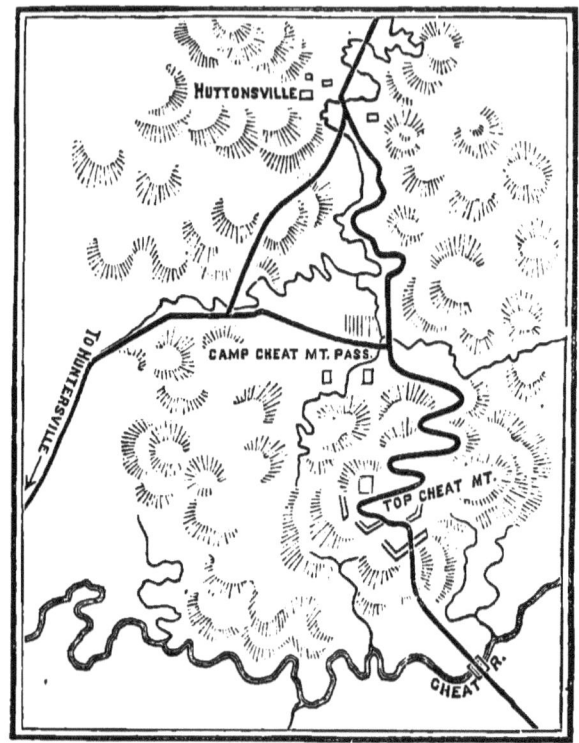

On the east side of the camp was the pass out of the valley. Upon the highest peak, from the tallest pine-tree, waved the Stars and Stripes.

On the 28th, by order of General Reynolds, Clark, Johnston, and myself explored the mountains on the east, to find if it was possible for the enemy to make any approach from that side. We found this wilderness of woods uninhabited and inaccessible, except to deer and bear, or the most energetic scouts.

In the evening I examined a few men who resided southward among the mountains, and who were fleeing from the Rebels, as Union men. I drew from their description a map, giving every house, and the name and supposed sentiments of the inhabitants.

On the morning of the 29th of July, General Reynolds and staff went up the mountain to the camp and fortifications situated on the top. The day was very pleasant. The road is good, — winding, serpent-like, up the mountain-side. Large trees, overhanging, shut out the sky above, and looking downward, we see tree-tops pointing upward to us. We can see the camp of Cheat Mountain Pass, like a map, in the valley. The river winds away into the hidden passes that give it outlet to the country beyond. The flag which, at the pass, seemed so high above us, now is a speck at our feet, which we can scarcely discern as it plays in the wild breeze. Up higher yet among the mist, and we arrive at the top. Here we find a level, where some bold farmer has located. Yes, on a mountain-top we find fertile fields and springs. This peculiarity of this branch of the Alleghany Mountains has given it the name of Rich Mountain Range. We spent some hours reviewing the works, and went to the very front and watered our horses in Cheat River. I thought what a pleasant trip it would be to start at its head-waters, and follow its foaming current to where it empties into the Monongahela.

I asked Clark where it came from. He replied it came from the "Big Spring," to whose waters were added a thousand other mountain springs, but the Big Spring, or "dividing waters," gave it birth.

"We will take a trip up that way some day," said I.

July 30th, Clark and I were arranging our tent, when Gen. Reynolds called us to him, and informed us that the enemy were supposed to be somewhere in the neighborhood of the Big Spring, and he wanted us to go out on the Huntersville road and learn the situation of the enemy. He ordered us to ride our horses as far as the pickets, and then go on foot, and to report to him by the next evening. It was then about 7 A. M., and one of the pleasantest days we had had. We were soon mounted. With a little hard bread in our pockets, and our revolvers in our belts, we were ready for a two days' scout. Clark had on a pair of dark pants, an army shirt, and a green flannel frock,— formerly a part of the uniform of the (Rebel) Washington Battery, which had been given to him by General Morris after the battle of Cheat River,— and a black felt hat, the worse for wear. I had put on a dark frock-coat of Clark's, a felt hat belonging to our ambulance-driver, and a pair of gray pants, also captured among Rebel uniforms at Cheat River.

After starting, Clark says, "Fletcher, I don't like this going on foot. Suppose we ask to go all the way, or as far as we choose, on our horses." "I am in the habit of obeying orders just to the letter without questioning, but will venture to ask a change in this case." So we rode back; but the General did not change his order, and away we went. On the road leading southwest from camp, and right up Tygart's Valley River, which we cross and recross any number of times, we saw some men lounging by Conrad's Mills, and asked a few questions, which were answered in a manner that led us to think they were "Secesh." An hour's ride and we came to the picket, six miles out. We gave an officer of the picket General Reynolds's order to move four miles further and take charge of our horses.

We left our horses with the picket, by a little log house, which had long been deserted, or perhaps had been built for a country school-house, and so little used that trees had grown up under the eaves, hiding it from view.

After firing off our revolvers and reloading, we started off down the road. Passing a few deserted farms, we found the country more broken, the valley narrower, and the river crossing and recrossing the road every few yards. Soon we came to a little farm-house, where a young man was mending a harrow near the door.

"Can we get dinner here?" I asked. "I reckon," was the reply. We then had some conversation about the country. He said the "Yankees had taken his corn, and paid him for it in Ohio money, which he could not use. But he did not seem inclined to speak out his Rebel feelings, as he did not know how we stood. His wife came to the door; she was of the dish-rag and broomstick sort.

"How long will it be till we have dinner?" Mr. Clark asked. "Jist when you git it," said she, going into the house, saying something about "nasty Yankees." We moved on, giving up all idea of dinner at that house. Some two miles brought us to another cabin, where we found a native, with a wife and nine children, — the oldest about sixteen, — and all living in one small room. Each had a corn-cob pipe; — even the baby was playing with one.

The old lady made us some corn-cake, and fried some salt pork, to which we did full justice.

This man lived on neutral ground, which neither Yankees nor Rebels frequented, and he seemed to have no opinions himself; in fact, he knew as little as most of the wild men of West Virginia, — nothing but what some cross-road stump-speaker had said. He knew nothing of the country beyond; a high bluff near the house he had never been on, and thought there might be a "heap of rattlesnakes" up there. We paid for our dinner, and once more bent our steps southward. The scenery was grand, the valley lonesome, the road and river winding across each other at the very bottom of the narrow valley. We met no one, and saw but one man, who, of course, knew nothing by nature and less by cultivation, till we came into a little settlement, at Mingo Flats, where we saw three women standing in the door of a rather respectable-looking frame-house. It was near 5 P. M., and we were quite tired, — I, at least. I asked if we could stay all night. They told us that we could find a good place a few miles further on. They asked if we were soldiers, and from which army, and seemed very kind. We asked if any of the Confederates had been there lately. They said, none for two weeks; they had all gone into camp at Huntersville; and, in answer to our inquiry, it was four miles to the Big Spring, where we could stay all night.

Bidding them good-night, we trudged on up a high hill, leaving the valley to our left. Our road was over mountain-spurs, and very tedious travelling. Some two miles further on, we noticed the tracks of horses, — fresh ones, too, — and the mark of a pistol-ball on an oak-tree. We now began to look sharply about us, for we knew that Rebel Cavalry had been there.

The sinking sun had now cast the mountain-shadow upon our path, and the way was more gloomy. I was so tired, it was only by slow walking and great effort I could follow, — stopping here and there to listen, or still oftener to drink from the springs which all along come gurgling up from the rocks. A fever seemed working in my veins. My companion and I had talked freely all day, but now both were silent. We had stopped for a moment, when we heard a horseman coming toward us; and, looking up the narrow road, saw a native, with an old horse, and a green hunting-shirt on, coming up. We stopped him and asked the distance to the "Big Spring." He thought it was about two miles. He said he had seen no one on the road; no soldiers had been in these parts for more than two weeks.

We started on, my companion wishing to go from the road and take to the forest; but the craggy appearance was uninviting to my weary limbs, and I said, "No; let us keep the path till we come to a more level spot." So on we went. I thrust my staff into the damp ground, wondering if I would take it up again in the morning. The road was beginning a gentle descent; the last gleams of the sun tinged the high mountain-tops and the clouds before us. A death-like stillness pervaded the scene around us, broken only by the note of a solitary whippoorwill and the sound of our own steps, which seemed to fall heavy on the damp ground. Directly in front of us, at a distance of a hundred yards, stood a large oak-tree.

My companion came to a halt. "I saw a man move behind that tree. Let us take to the woods, and go around." "No; I think you are mistaken. I can make out any form I wish to on dark and shadowy evenings. I think it's imagination."

He fell back near me, and we approached the spot, I almost heedlessly; and just as we neared the oak, — "Halt! Halt! Halt!" greeted us from every bush, tree, stump, and stone. My companion, who was watching for this very thing, leaped backward, with his revolver drawn, ready for battle.

The ambuscade was well laid, for just here was an open space, where it was much lighter than any place along the road. "What are you stopping citizens here for, in the public highway?" said I. "Surrender!" said a tall Rebel, who seemed to be in command, and who had a long deer-rifle, with hair-trigger, levelled at my breast. (I could hear my companion saying, in a low voice, "Run, Fletcher, run!") "What do you want of us? What will you do if we surrender?" "Only take you to camp; and then, if you are all right, let you go." "Run, Clark, run!" said I: "I can't." "Just you stand still. If your friend moves, I'll blow you to h—l!" said the tall Alabamian. I looked about me; bayonets and old rifles were looking at me. I felt too tired to attempt a leap into the bushes, and saying, "I surrender!" threw my revolver on the ground. Clark lowered his, which had been pointed at the tall man all the time,* and said, "I'll go with you, then."

Approaching me, he said, in a whisper almost, "What shall we tell them?" "Truth only, and as little as possible." So, under guard, without arms, we were marched down a winding way, a mile perhaps, when we heard laughter and singing, and soon came in sight of a two-story log house, with steps up the outside to the first floor. We were at the "Big Spring," our intended destination; but this was not our intended condition.

"Who is you all?" said a half-dozen voices, and a crowd of homespun fellows crowded around us.

We refused to answer questions except to the commanding officer, who soon made his appearance in the shape of a plain, honest-looking man, Captain Bird, of the Sixth Alabama Regiment. "Where are you from, men?" "We are soldiers from the Federal Army, — were out scouting under orders, — and walked into your ambuscade." I gave also my real name and rank. Turning to Mr. Clark, he asked his name and what State he was from. "I am from Wood County, Virginia. My name is Leonard Clark. I am a soldier in the

---

* Mr. Clark did not fire, because he knew it would cause my death; and gave himself up, — "For," said he, "I never could live happy had I left you in that time of trouble."

Union Army." "Don't you know, sir," said a Rebel officer who stood by, stepping up in an excited manner,—"don't you know you are guilty of the most damnable treason, taking up arms against your native State, and leading the Yankee Abolitionists to our homes, to burn our houses, and rape our women, and steal our niggers? I'll cut your damned heart out!" and he made a pass at Clark with his drawn sword. "I am your prisoner. I demand to be treated as a prisoner of war." "You do not deserve to be treated as a prisoner of war—but as a black-hearted traitor to your State. Did n't you know, sir, that your State was voted out of the Union? and you have no right to serve against her."

"I know," said Clark, standing like a statue, firm and fearless, with an eye fixed on his accuser, which made him fear and tremble,—"I know Virginia—free Virginia—is now said to be out of the Union; but Virginia is only ruled by despotism, and was voted out by force." I shall never forget the tableau which ensued after this speech. The crowd which seemed ready to tear him to pieces was only held back by the iron face which showed no change, and the eye that flashed truth and fearlessness. But a pang of sorrow came, for I saw that Clark's position was one even worse than my own;—he would find persons who knew him, and enemies who would like to condemn him; but I was unknown, and did not fear meeting any one.

We were taken up the old wooden stairway, and put into the room which was occupied by the soldiers. Captain Bird said they could not give us much to eat, as they had just come there, and their baggage had not come up. Some cornbread and a tin-cup full of coffee were given us. I remarked I'd rather have Lincoln bread, and took some of our hard bread from my pocket, which amused the fellows very much; they wanted a bit of it, to keep as a trophy. My papers, map, &c. were still in my pocket, and weighed on my mind. On the fire-shelf was a corn-cob pipe. I filled it, and drawing my papers out, stripped them through my hand slowly, as though to make a lighter, and, touching them to the blaze, puffed away till all were burned, without attracting any attention. We were surrounded by a crowd of curious questioners. I talked with the intention of amusing, and created quite a laugh occasionally. Clark was silent.

Two women came in to see the Yankees, — wives of officers, I suppose. They were quite bitter in their remarks. They knew we were spies, and had no doubt our capture prevented our poisoning the spring, and murdering the babes of women whose husbands were gone to the war.

Two guards were stationed at the door. The soldiers threw themselves on the floor each side of us, and all became quiet within; but outside I could hear the clatter of horses and the striking of sabres and stirrups. I saw Captain Bird pass through the room with papers, and heard him order the guard to be doubled, and every man be on the lookout. And then I heard the horsemen dash off. All became still again, except occasional crackling of the dying embers in the huge old fireplace, and the low whispering of the guard at the door. I could hear them speculate as to our future, — whether we were really spies or not, — and if we would be shot or hung. "I would like to put a hole through that d—d fellow in the green jacket," said one. "I'll bet I could whip ten Yankees like that smart fellow that thinks he can laugh it all off. I'll bet he'll swing." Such was the conversation of the night, whenever I roused up from a sleep made horrid by dreams. But, thank God, morning came at last. I wanted to be moving. What I dreaded most was time, — like a boy dreading a whipping, — more dreadful by delay. I wanted events to transpire with rapidity.

Early morning, and everything seemed like a dream. I was taken out by a guard of three men to the Big Spring, which gushes out of the rocks in a stream as large as a man's body. I bathed my aching head in its cold waters. As the bubbles danced under my eye, I thought, O that I could dance and whirl on the sparkling stream down Cheat River, where I stood two days before with Clark, asking where the Big Spring was. I saw that we were to be closely watched, — three or four guards with each of us wherever we went. I noticed a Rebel lieutenant in the house as I returned, who had been our prisoner a few weeks before; he had been paroled by McClellan, and was now here, apparently on duty.

After a breakfast of cold corn-bread, we were marched out in front of the cabin, and Captain Bird ordered a squad of men to guard us. " It's customary," said he, " to tie our prisoners; but if you will promise not to attempt to escape, you shall not be tied." " It is not customary," said I, " to tie our prisoners; your men captured by us were hardly guarded; but if you think six armed and mounted men can't guard us, you must have little confidence in them." After searching us, and taking every article from us except a small drinking-cup which I had, and our clothing, we were told that we were going to be sent to head-quarters, — that we were captured under very suspicious circumstances.

He (Captain Bird) then charged the mounted guard, who were to take us, to march us between them; not to let us talk; and to shoot us if we attempted to move from the road. Thus we left the Big Spring, — six horsemen, armed with old horse-pistols and double-barrelled shot-guns, as an escort. We found the country very wild, as we went southward, and noticed that we were almost constantly descending steep hills, while the day before we were constantly ascending. During the forenoon we met long trains of wagons and hundreds of soldiers, all going on up toward the Spring.

Clark and I both felt our situation was one which would need great patience, for the insulting remarks of many as they passed were almost unbearable. Sometimes we were permitted to ride a short distance behind some of the men. At noon, after we had descended a very steep hill, we came into a beautiful valley, where we found a large camp of about four thousand men. The situation of the camp was most beautiful, and the grounds were kept very clean and closely guarded.

The sergeant marched us around to the south side, where we were halted before the tent of Colonel Lee, — a son of Major-General Lee. The sergeant dismounted, went into his tent, and the Colonel came to the door with some papers in his hand, from which he read, and then looked at us sharply for a moment, while I looked as sharply in return. He was a man of medium size; hair and beard a little sprinkled with gray. His face indicated great sternness. He gave some orders to a major, who said to me, "I shall be obliged to put you in irons." At the same time an orderly produced a pair of those unbecoming and uncomfortable jewels, which he began to unlock to put on.

"Is it customary to put captured soldiers in irons?" said I.

"You have heard of the battle of Bull Run, have n't you? Well, these irons were captured by our men from you Yankees. You intended to put them on our men and march them to Richmond, but we intend to make every Yankee wear them that we capture."

While I put out my wrist for the cursed fetters, I told the major that I did not believe one word of any handcuffs being captured.

He assured me it was so, and that all the officers of the Yankee army had their baggage marked "Richmond, Va." He also informed us that General Scott was captured, and his fine carriage, etc., etc. All the Southern brag that could be brought up, he furnished on this occasion.

This camp is, or was, known as Edri, — half-way between Big Springs and Huntersville.

After our irons were secure, Clark and I both wristed together, we were taken by a guard to a brick house, which was quite large, and put in an upper room, on the outside of which two sentinels were placed. We sat on the floor some moments, when a man came in with some cold cornbread and milk. He took off the irons, that we might eat. He then retired.

Soon we heard a noise outside, as though some one was fighting, or trying to get away. The sound grew louder, and our door was unlocked, when a tall, well-dressed Virginian, heavily ironed, was thrown into our room, with apparent force. The door was again shut, and we three sat for a moment in silence; when our new fellow-prisoner said, "Don't give it up, men! I was captured at the same place you were, last night. I'm not going to back out for these d—d traitors; it a'n't my way. I've been leading Rosecrans and General McClellan, and I am not done yet! Where are you from, boys? Don't look down. We'll be even, by ——."

Come, be social. You don't say a word; you're scared, I suppose."

"We are not very badly scared," said I; "and as I have seen first-class players, real stars on the boards, I can't compliment your acting; you overdo it; and, besides, we are not trying to make many new acquaintances down here."

This seemed to act like a cold shower-bath. The sergeant (who, with others, had evidently been listening to us at the door) now came in and abused our new prisoner, in all the rough Southern cant phrases, for being a Union man; and finally took him out of the room by great force, as though to carry him to his execution. "Clark, we won't be caught by stool-pigeons."

About two P. M. we were ironed and put in an old wagon, with soldiers on each side, besides an escort of mounted men; and thus we travelled down the mountain slopes, through a wild country. We met two or three regiments marching up, and at the crossing of Greenbrier River some large wagon-trains, — all going one way, viz: up towards the Cheat Mountains. At last, just as the sun went down, we came through the pass into the little town of Huntersville, county seat of Pocahontas County.

Our escort seemed at a loss what to do with us, or where to leave us. So, driving up through the streets to the hotel, he gave us a good view of the camp, which was very large, situated all about the village. I think not less than seven thousand men must have been in this camp.

After we had been waiting some time in front of the hotel, where we were the centre of a crowd of curious questioners, and where Clark was recognized by some old acquaintances, we were driven back the road we had come, about a mile, to a camp of the Forty-second Virginia Regiment, Colonel Gilham* commanding; and here Clark and I were taken from the wagon, and marched off in different directions. I saw no more of him for several days. As for myself, I felt now miserable indeed to lose my companion in trouble. I had little time to grieve, however, before I was ushered into the

---

* Formerly Major Gilham, U. S. A., "of Indiana," alas! Author of a *Manual for Volunteers*, &c.

presence of Colonel Gilham, who, I believe, was in former years a professor in the Virginia Military Institute. He was a gentlemanly, kind-spoken man, and asked me many questions about the three-months' campaign. He then told me the latest news of the Bull Run battle, how badly we were whipped, &c. He informed me that news of our capture had been sent down the night before, and that we were to be examined as spies. He spoke very kindly; said he was sorry that one so young should be found in my condition. My only reply to all he said was, "I am perfectly satisfied, and don't need any sympathy." Colonel Gilham wanted me to tell him plainly what I was doing when I was captured, and what my rank was in our army. I answered that those who took me could answer his first question, and as to the latter, I had no rank. I was a soldier, on a scouting expedition. It was now quite dark. A storm was brewing in the mountains, and I was in hopes of being sent to some comfortable cell in the jail, but Colonel Gilham ordered a guard to take me up to headquarters. So a tall fellow, real F. F. V., in a gray uniform, which had any number of yards of gold lace and buttons on, marched on one side, and a soft-clay-eater, from Georgia, on the other. I was marched up to the centre of the town to the hotel, up an old stairway to a large room, where sat an Orderly, who informed some one in the inner room, in rather a loud voice, " That Yankee spy is here, General." " Send him in: send him in. Put a strong guard at the door, also at the windows outside. Take off his irons, too, and let no one in till I call." I was taken in. At a long table, covered with maps and papers, sat a little man, a Malay in form and complexion, and a demon in countenance; he had but one arm, black hair, and dead eyes looking out from withered eyebrows. Placing a large revolver before him, he motioned me to sit down on the other side of the table. I did so.

" What is your name, young man?" I told him, and asked, " Whom have I the honor of speaking with?" " You, sir, are in the presence of General Loring, late of the United States Army, but now of the Confederate Army."

General Loring kept me some two hours, questioning me

and trying to puzzle me; he was particularly anxious to get from me some knowledge of our strength and position on Cheat Mountain, — at times persuading, at times threatening. He said, "Before to-morrow's sun goes down, I'll hang you both. Your only hope for mercy is in confessing *all, all* you know." "General, you have the hanging power, I admit; but wouldn't it set a bad example to our army to begin hanging soldiers who fall into your hands?"

General Loring was unkind, insulting, abusive, with nothing of the gentleman or soldier in him. Late in the night he ordered the guard to take me back to camp. Tired, footsore, and hungry, I reached Colonel Gilham's quarters, where he ordered a negro to give me some corn-bread and meat. After eating, I fell asleep. I was roused up by falling from a log on which I had been sitting. I found three men guarding me, and the rain pouring down. How long I had been asleep, I can't tell; but a new guard came on duty, and brought an old tent, which they put up for me; and into which they thrust me. Without straw or cover, I lay on the soaking ground.

Since the days of the deluge, I do not think it has stormed so hard and long; rain either fell by night or day, for the next six weeks; seldom more than two or three hours of sunshine, till the torrents came down. Colonel Gilham's camp was in what had been a cornfield, and the water came pouring down the old furrows, and through the tent above. I was most terribly cold all night, the more so as my feet were tied with a rope, which was held by the guard at the door. The night was passed in as great mental as physical agony. In the morning, at about ten o'clock, a negro brought some corn-bread and fried pork, which made me very sick. Crowds of men stood there in the rain, looking in at me and making all sort of remarks about my personal appearance, and conjecturing what my feelings were. None could talk with me, except officers who got permits from General Loring. A few came in, only to provoke me into saying something by abuse, as by reading the outrageous lies about Bull Run.

The topic which all the officers and soldiers seemed inclined to talk about was, when, how, and where we were to be executed.

The second day at Huntersville, I was taken again before General Loring. This time General Robert E. Lee was in command; he had arrived that day. General Loring began by asking the direction in which we had come, and many of the same questions asked before. General Lee then said, —

"Young man, how long have you been soldiering?"

"Three months, General."

"Were you persuaded to go into the army, or did you choose it?"

"I went in *because of the cause.*"

"Have the people of Indiana confidence in Governor Morton? Can he get those six regiments into the field again?"

"General, what I say to you, I know is true. Governor Morton had to turn off thousands and thousands of men, at the first call for Volunteers. The six regiments have gone home, to be sure, but it is only to be better armed and equipped, and to spread the fire, the military patriotic contagion, into every heart."

"How many men from Indiana are in the field?"

"As I said before, General, I was a three-months' man. I do not know how many are in the field now; but if the men of Indiana were to see me here in irons, and then remember the treatment of prisoners at Cheat River and Laurel Hill and Rich Mountain, a hundred thousand men would be in arms to-morrow, and Governor Morton at their head."

"I shall not let you talk so," said General Loring.

"Remember, you were not taken in battle," said General Lee; "if you were, you would not be in irons."

After a long conversation about Generals McClellan, Rosecrans, Morris, and Reynolds, in which he desired a minute personal description, he said, —

"Young man, we will have to keep you very close, very safe, until we can get the evidence of those who captured you."

When I was marched back to the tent, a mile off, I got a good view of Huntersville; and if a sheep-skin, just taken

9

off, were spread on the ground, with the tail southwest, the head northeast, it would convey a very good idea of the shape of the valley in which the town is situated. The mountains rise on all sides, leaving but four gaps, through which pass the roads. It is impossible for any one to come into or go out of the town without going through these passes, or climbing the rough mountains. The town contains a few old frame buildings, one church, now used as a hospital, (in fact, every house almost was a hospital at this time,) also a brick hotel, now head-quarters, a brick courthouse and a jail, two-stories, side by side, and not unlike.

In the valley, and up the mountain-slopes, were camps; and every day new men were coming in. Alabama had two or three regiments; Tennessee had the Seventh, Fourteenth, and Sixteenth; Virginia, the Forty-second and others, — I could not get the number; Georgia, the Sixteenth and others, — number not ascertained; also the Rockbridge Cavalry, and a company of Mississippians, mounted as Rangers. In all, my estimate of General Lee's forces amounted to over eleven thousand men. This knowledge, and the fact that General Reynolds had but a handful at Cheat Mountain, with his works unfinished, made me fear that Lee might advance immediately; but, thank God, our capture had this one good result, of delaying his advance for more than six weeks.

Both Clark and myself had refused to answer questions in regard to our numbers and our artillery force, except that we admitted having seen some ten or twelve large guns, and a few howitzers, but knew nothing of the number of infantry, beyond "some ten regiments which we saw on the road."

After more than a week at Camp Gilham, the Forty-second Virginia Regiment was ordered to the front, and I was moved to the camp of the Fourteenth Tennessee, where I was happy to be once more in prison with Clark. We were in a tent by ourselves, very closely guarded, with orders not to speak to each other nor to any one else, except when permitted to do so by the officer of the guard. We found the Tennesseeans much kinder than the Virginians. Nothing of importance transpired here. The usual remarks and brag, so characteristic of Southerners, were gone through by almost every man. Some of the officers were gentlemen in their deportment, but the men were ignorant and sometimes unkind; although when our feet were to be tied at night, almost every man who had the duty to perform, apologized, saying he was sorry, but it had to be done, as he was obeying orders.

One Sunday, the chaplain of the regiment came in to talk with us in regard to our spiritual state. He asked us if we were "prepared to die." "As far as we knew, we had no further preparation to make."

"Did we think we were doing right to come down South to lead the Yankees to murder Southern innocence?" We thought he was partly mistaken as to our purpose; nevertheless we thought we were doing right. "Did we know the end that awaited us?" "No, not exactly; we did n't know just how cruel and barbarous it might be, but supposed that it would be all right, whatever it was." In fact, we expected nothing good of any one, and did n't seem to object to being hung, either. So our chaplain left us.

I do not remember how long we were in this regiment. We were poorly fed, but had good water; no covering was given us, nor straw to lie upon. We were transferred to the safe-keeping of the Sixteenth Georgia Regiment; and a meaner, more cowardly, ignorant, and infernal set of heathen were never assembled together. My friend Clark had been sick for more than a week; I could see his health failing; he was so weak he could hardly walk; he had fever night and day; — yet these villains tied him hand and foot at night, and caused us to lie upon the wet ground. They furnished us with rations unfit for dogs, and brought us water that the filthiest hog would shrink from wallowing in.

One night I said to the officer of the guard, "Please, do not tie this man to-night; he has been too ill to rise all day, and the surgeon refuses to come."

"He's a d—d traitor, and has said he could whip any two men in our camp; and d—d if he shall have any favors of me!"

"I know, sir, this is false: we are not allowed to speak;

and I know he did not make boast or threat of any kind. I will ask to be doubly ironed and tied, and if Clark should move or do or say anything displeasing, just hang me in the morning."

"No more of your d—d nonsense," said he, coming in with the rope, and beginning to tie Clark.

"It is my opinion, sir, that the boast of manliness and generosity and noble feeling in the South is all humbug. There is not a man in the North so mean and cowardly as to do this act."

"D—— you! Perhaps you think I won't tie you, too?"— for as I was not considered physically dangerous, and as they supposed I knew nothing of the country, they often left me untied.

"I don't care what you do," said I, excitedly, losing my temper for the first time. "You are mean enough to do most anything." He did tie me, and that tightly, from head to foot, so that the marks were on me for two days.

Hundreds of Confederate soldiers died at Huntersville, of measles and camp-diarrhœa. Clark and I suffered with the latter.

To add to our misery, two lousy Georgians, who had been found asleep on picket, were put in prison with us, where they cried and whimpered like sick girls, day and night, for fear of being shot. Thank heaven, the Sixteenth Georgia were ordered on, and we once more changed camp. We inquired what State our new regiment was from, and were delighted to learn it was the Sixteenth Tennessee, Colonel Savage commanding, and that it was now the only regiment in Huntersville. We were put into the guard-tent, along with three or four West Virginia men, who were charged with disloyalty.

Many unpleasant restrictions were removed. We could talk; we could stand outside the tent, and enjoy various other small liberties. But this state of things did not last long. A mean little lawyer came around and got the supposed Union men released. Having nothing further to do, he must hurry up Clark's case before the authorities. 'Squire Skeen was prosecuting attorney for the State.

One evening, near sundown, I was taken under guard to General Donelson's quarters; for he had arrived, and was the commanding officer. His tent was pitched in a beautiful grove. The venerable old man, with his gray locks combed behind his ears, sat in the door, smoking his pipe. He was exceedingly polite. He talked with me a long time. He had been at Indianapolis, attending some Democratic convention. He knew that Indiana had a majority in favor of Southern Rights. Yes, he remembered a young man there, who was a remarkable man, too, — a genius; he met him at the Palmer House; he knew he must be on the right side.

"What was his name, General? Perhaps I know him."

"I think," said the General, "his name is Ryan, — Richard Ryan."

"Yes, General, he is on the right side," said I. "I heard him make the hottest war-speech I ever listened to, the very night Fort Sumter fell."

"How uncertain men are!" said the General, thoughtfully.

Mr. Skeen then questioned and cross-questioned me in regard to Clark. There were two men, strangers, writing down my answers. Several men were examined who had known Clark at home, for years; and, with one voice, they said he was, at home, a steady, honest man, intelligent enough, but a strong Union man, and they had no doubt could do, and might have done, great harm to the Confederate cause. After this examination, I was taken over to the tent, accompanied by General Donelson's adjutant, whose name I think was Elliott. He was formerly connected with one of the Nashville papers; — I am not certain in regard to the name.

The moon was at its full, and had just rolled up over the eastern mountains, lighting up the valley with a pale glow, almost sufficient to read by. When I reached the tent, Clark asked me where I had been. I told him Skeen had brought some strangers there, and I had been examined as to my knowledge of him.

"They are going to kill us, Fletcher, — me, at any rate."

"Oh, no! don't get gloomy; they will not dare to kill us."

While we were talking, General Donelson and staff, and Colonel Savage and his staff-officers, rode up to the tent and ordered a guard to conduct the prisoners out into the field, beyond the camp. We went out. A crowd of men were watching, and followed as far as the guard-lines permitted. Clark and I stood side by side. Oh, how brightly the bayonets glitter in the cold moonlight; how heavily the soldiers tread; and how cold and uncheering is every sound!

We were halted in the middle of a large field. The officers stood, in consultation, fifty paces off. I looked up to the moon, that perhaps others, who had not forgotten us, might look at, too; — all the rest of the scene was ours alone.

Colonel Savage came up and said, " Prisoners, if you have anything to say, you must say it now, as you will never have another opportunity. You must hold all conversation in the presence of these officers."

I turned to Clark. " Well, Clark, I am sorry to part with one who became a prisoner to save my life. Your life as a prisoner, under all your trials and tortures, has shown you to be ever the same brave, unwavering, honorable man. Whatever may be our future, I respect and love you. We shall meet again, but till then good-bye. If you ever have a chance, let some of our men know where I am; and if I have a chance, I will do the same."

Mr. Clark said: " Fletcher, I am not sorry that I gave myself up to save you. I feel that you are a true man. If you ever get home, see my wife and children; tell her to do for them as I intended to do. I am not afraid to die for my country. This is all I wish to say."

" Return these men to separate quarters, Colonel," said General Donelson; " and do not permit them to speak to each other."

Colonel Savage did not separate us, however, but ordered the guard doubled; and we promised to be quiet. Neither of us slept that night. Clark felt that we were going to be sent away to some other prison. I told him I thought the whole thing was foolery, to get us to say something which would condemn us.

But morning came, and just as we were getting our breakfast, four mounted men rode up, hurried Clark out without allowing one parting word, and I saw them bind him to the horse with chain and rope. While I stood there, my heart almost sank within me, but it roused up enough to heap a heavy and audible curse upon the proceeding, which caused me to be kept inside the tent and tied likewise. I now became cross and sick. I gave few kind words to any one who spoke to me. I made up my mind to escape. Twice before I might have done so, but for leaving Clark when he was sick; now nothing kept me back but guns. I could get out, and I would. Next day, after making this resolve, our camp was moved up on higher ground on the mountain-side southwest of the town. Here I was so poorly fed, or so sick, that I began to think I would die of fever. All day long I lay at the door of the tent. Across the mountain-tops, wrapt in clouds and Indian-summer haze, was my dream-land. Oh, how I longed to cross the wilderness, to give Reynolds notice of the foe that was threatening his front and crawling in his rear; how I prayed in feverish dreams that some spiritual communication might reveal to him his danger! I fixed in my own mind how Lee would draw Reynolds out for battle on the 'pike, near Cheat River or Greenbrier Bridge, and then fall with his larger force on the flank and rear. So, after days of waiting, I slipped my irons one stormy night, and making my way out of the tent by lifting the curtain at the back, I followed a little path down through the now almost desolate camp, for all but one regiment had gone on. I was just making my way cautiously along, between two tall pines, when I ran against the sentinel, who was standing there to keep out of the rain. He was more frightened than I, but he was kind enough to keep still. He told me I was a fool for trying to get away; I would die before I could get to our lines. I gave it up for that night, got into my tent the way I got out, and no one was wiser in the morning.

Next day an old man was put in prison with me; he was one of the wealthiest farmers in Greenbrier County. He was seventy-two years old, and was imprisoned because, at the time the vote was cast for testing Virginia's choice as to Secession or Union, he voted for the old Union. The old man was very cold at night and had a terrible cough. I wrote several notes to General Donelson, telling him that we had no clothing, little food, and no way to cook it. He answered, in the most polite manner, that he would order the evils remedied, but he never did. This old gentleman, Alexander Mann by name, was released a few weeks afterwards, upon his sons coming over and joining the Rebel Army. One of the young men came into the tent to see his father, and as a gift brought his pocket full of potatoes, which I think were the only vegetables I tasted in Western Virginia.

Perhaps it was two weeks before I made another attempt to escape. I succeeded in passing the Rebel guard-lines, and was well round the valley toward the place where I intended striking into the mountains, when I heard signal-guns firing, which were answered by shots all along the outposts. I knew no pains would be spared to retake me, for they had often told me that any attempt to escape would be followed by a speedy hanging as a spy. They knew well the damage I could do.

On I went, through the tangled laurel-bushes, over broken ledges, up slippery steeps, down through tangled ravines, cold streams, and marshes, the rain pouring down in torrents, and only a dim ray of light through the midnight sky. At length I dragged my weary and chilled limbs up the mountain which so long had seemed to shut my view from the old flag waving on Cheat Mountain. Some pickets or patrols, who were kept out on these mountains to prevent negroes from running off, came down not far from me, and I think either saw or heard me, or perhaps their dogs scented me; at last, I heard them returning. 'T is painful to write the tortures of that night, toiling up the ascent, which in the daytime, from a distance, seemed so smooth, like a sugar loaf, rising from a broad base, sloping gently to a round apex, but which I found to be as rough and wild as any other mountain. Till morning I toiled like one in a horrid nightmare, trying to get over the Summit, away from my pursuers, but always coming back to the same place. As daylight dawned, I stretched my wearied and torn limbs in a thick jungle of laurels, upon the moss-covered rocks; and there I lay all day. I could look southwest into the camp, across the little town. I could see convalescent soldiers crawling about in the sun, like flies after a frosty morning. But from headquarters I could see mounted men dash off by every road, and scouts coming toward the very mountain I was on.

Looking northeast, the scene was one unbroken wilderness of wood and cloud-capped mountains. I formed my plans for the next night's march. I had saved enough fat pork (which I had tied round me with my shoe-strings) to keep me alive, with the help of wild fruit, for four days' travelling.

I was to descend the mountain northeast at its base. I was to follow up a brawling stream which had cut its bed through the rocks. I was to follow it for six miles; then strike across another mountain to Greenbrier River, which I expected to follow up for some twenty miles; until I could strike north to Cheat Mountain.

When night came, dim but starlit, I made my way down the mountain, and keeping in the water of the little stream, had gone perhaps two miles when I heard "Halt, halt!" from the bank above, followed by two or three shots. This only increased my speed up the slippery rocks, fighting the dashing water. I climbed like a madman. Just as I turned under a shelving cliff, "Halt!" said a strong voice, — "Halt!" A sentinel fired, — so near, I could have touched the end of his gun; but on I went up the rocks as if up a stairway, the foaming current dashing against me, — the sentinel close behind me with fixed bayonet. I turned with a spring, threw myself down upon him, hoping to throw him down and get his arms. I was received on the point of his bayonet, which penetrated my left hip, striking to the bone. I fell to the water. He grasped me by the clothing and lifted me to one side, saying, in an excited manner, "Fletcher, are you hurt?" "Yes." "Can you get up?" "No." My only thought was, What will become of our men at Cheat Mountain. What a fool was I for trying to get out of the valley that way! Why did n't I start out in some other direction?

While I thus reflected, the other men came down and, making a litter, carried me back in triumph to my old quarters. As I passed by the tent of a sneaking second lieutenant, he stood, with a torch in his hand, to have a look at me. "Did you wound him?" said he to the guard. "Yes." "Well, you might as well have killed him, for he knew, if he ever attempted to get away, he would be hung." This was too much for me to take from the insulting scoundrel, and for the second time I let fly at him,—"Hang and be d—d to your whole cowardly crew!"

Next morning I was visited by Colonel Savage, who questioned me as to why and how I made my escape. The getting off my irons he could not understand,—thought some one did it for me, and wound up by saying, "If you don't tell the clean thing, I'll send you to the jail."

"Colonel, I have desired to go to jail ever since I came into this cursed community. I have had to sleep for two months, almost, without clothing or straw. I have never had water enough to wash hands or face. I have had to eat uncooked rations very often,—and only the meagerest and meanest rations at that."

"Take him to jail, Lieutenant. See how he likes his change of quarters."

In half an hour I had an opportunity of examining one of those tight institutions which some men build to put other men in. In the centre of the two-story brick building was a heavy oak door. We walk into an entry or hall. At our right is an oak door filled with spikes, and furnished with a large hasp and padlock. The jailer is an old man, with long white hair, which he combs upward to cover the bald crown. He has on a dirty white shirt, a pair of jean breeches, and a pair of old shoes, cut down at the heel and out at the toes, which only half hide his stockingless feet; his face is as wrinkled as the crumply skims on boiled milk; and his nose and chin approach each other so closely, I venture to say, although he is evidently a shoemaker, he has no need of pincers. He is sitting at his bench when we come in, pegging an old boot; he looks up, lays down the boot, looks at me, wipes his nose on the back of his hand, and then performs the same motion on his leathern apron.

"Well, you got de Yankee, did you?"

"Yes. Where shall I put him?"

"Oh, I'll fix that. There is the debtors' room empty.

Better put him in there. The cell's full already: got a runaway nig' and Moses in there. They expect the Yank' in there; but he's so sick-looking-like, I hate to."

"Never mind," said the Lieutenant;* "that's just the kind he likes. Them Abolitionists don't mind sleeping with niggers; and 'Mose' is as good as he."

The old jailer took down two keys from a nail in the wall, unlocked the padlock, threw back the oak door, and then a door, made of heavy iron cross-bars, presented itself. I tried to see into the cell, while he fumbled away at the lock, but it was too dark within. "I hardly ever unlock this door, and it's mighty rusty." Soon the door swung back, shrieking on its rusty hinges. Putting irons on was hard, but I shall never forget my repugnance at passing into that cell, and hearing the iron door slam, and the lock grind. And on this disgusting period it is painful to dwell. Hundreds came to look through at me, but I kept myself hid as much as possible.

By kindness I soon won the confidence of the negro "Jim," and the poor idiot "Mose."

Jim waited on me: he brushed my clothes with an old broom, and tried to black my rusty old shoes by using soot from the flue. When the jailer thrust the old wooden tray under the trap-door, Jim set it before me, and he made Mose wait till I had eaten. Mose was a poor idiot boy, nineteen years old, who had been in this filthy place for months.

The cell was about fourteen feet long and twelve feet wide; two small double-grated windows let in the little light we enjoyed by day; but early in the evening the heavy shutters were closed, and all was dark as pitch. At this time, I felt much like the fish that jumped from the frying-pan into the fire, for when I was in the tent, although I suffered from cold and rain, I could not complain of being stinted in the article of pure air; but I now suffered for want of it. It was my custom to lie on the floor with my face as close to the very small crack under the trap-door as possible.

* This Lieutenant was shortly afterward captured by our men. He told them that I was well treated and on parole in Huntersville, for which information Lieutenant Delzell and all the boys in Bracken's Cavalry paid him every kind attention.

In the morning, the guard came and opened the shutters, and life was tolerable till evening.

Many citizens — men, women, and children — came to see me. On Sunday I was more than crowded with visitors, who stood at the iron door, gaping like so many moon-struck toads. Very seldom would I talk with them; and I asked the guard, who were detailed from the militia, not to allow so many fools in the hall. Jim used to take his stand at the door and do all the talking, as the keeper of wild animals stands by their cage and explains where they were caught, how trained, and their habits. So Jim told about the Yankee, often spreading on to the story, which he manufactured, some of the most wonderful traits that a man ever had.

Jim was anxious to get out: so was I; and we began to work on the east window. When people came about, Jim talked to them, and whistled and sung, to deaden the noise of cutting and sawing with my knife, which I was using as cold-chisel and file on a bar of iron. We worked some every day, but the knife was worn out before the bar was half off.

Part of my time I spent in teaching Jim and Moses their letters, by drawing them on the floor with bits of charcoal. Jim learned very quickly, but Moses made no progress. The jailer's daughter let me have a few books. "Paul and Virginia," "Elizabeth; or the Exiles of Siberia," "John Wesley's Sermons," "A History of Marion and his Men," etc., etc., were all eagerly devoured, for they were more than companions to me now. Every book was a friend.

During all this time I was growing thinner and weaker every day. I could not sleep at night, for the foul air was poison to me. My head ached and my heart burned. In one of these sad midnight hours, dark to me but bright moonlight outside, I heard the guard, who were off duty, sing out, in full, rich strains, an old Methodist tune which I had heard years ago at camp-meeting, commencing with —

> "There is a place where my hopes are stayed;
> My heart and my treasure are there."

With this song the flood-gates of pent-up feeling burst, and for the first time tears washed down my fevered cheeks. Thoughts of home and friends occupied the rest of the night.

At length, my days at Huntersville came to an end. One Sunday afternoon I heard that a big battle was going on at Cheat Mountain, and that thousands of Yankees had been killed and captured the day before. The prisoners were to arrive at Huntersville that afternoon. Crowds of people occupied the court-house yard and the streets, waiting to see the " Yanks." I stood with my feet on the back of a chair, and my hands holding to the iron bar above me, peering out, trembling with excitement. Just at sunset I could see men coming through the mountain-pass, and, as they came nearer, I beheld the blue uniforms of the Union soldiers. On they came, and were drawn up in line, about two hundred yards from the jail. Would they be sent on without my having a chance to speak with them, to find the truth? Would I be sent on with them?

I walked back and forth. I pounded on the door till the jailer came.

" Who is the officer in command of this town, this jail? What am I left here for?"

" I don't know anything about it. I was told to keep you till called for."

" I wish you would send the commandant of this post this note,"—and I handed him a scrap upon which I had asked to see the commandant.

In an hour a captain, in the Confederate service, who had once been in the regular army as lieutenant, came in, asked my name, rank, and regiment, and some other questions; then he ordered me to be put in a better place, the debtors' room, and said I should be sent on to Richmond the next morning, with the other prisoners. I did not sleep that night. I wanted to move—anywhere, anywhere, so that I was not lying still. I prayed that wherever Clark was, I might be sent, for since the day he was sent off, I had had that one desire above all others, to know where he was and be with him.

Next morning I was taken out to the table, breakfasted with the jailer's family, and then was returned to my quarters. How long that day seemed. At four P. M., a guard came. The door was thrown open. I walked across the hall, and shook hands with Jim and Moses. Both, with tears in their eyes, wished me good luck, and I was off. Oh, how soft and balmy seemed the air; how quiet and free everything seemed! I was surprised to find that I could hardly move my limbs: a walk of two hundred yards seemed like as many miles. I said nothing, for I was bound to leave Huntersville. We came to an orchard, where the Yankees were drawn up in line. They were ready to march. I dragged myself along as fast as possible. I looked each man in the face, in hopes to get one glance of recognition. One or two of the Sixth Ohio boys I recognized, but they did n't know me. Every one of them looked at me with wondering eyes. The end of the column was reached, where I was to march, when a young man stepped up to me, looking me in the face. "My God," said he, "is this Dr. Fletcher?"

"Yes," said I: "it is what remains of him."

Captain Bense came up; and Corporal Frank Kistler, of the Thirteenth Indiana, who had recognized me, introduced me, saying "that he had heard of me before."

"Fall in! Fall in!" shouted the Rebel lieutenant, who had us in charge. "Forward, march!" and away we went, Frank Kistler by my side, — who told me that only a picket party had been captured, and that Reynolds would "lam the Rebs like h—l." Then he told me the late news, but in few words, for no talking was allowed. In another hour, Huntersville was at our backs, and we were plodding along through the mountain-roads, wading deep, cold streams, and climbing up steep hills. My feet were a mass of blisters, and I was so weary that I would have given up; but I knew I would be sent back. I told Kistler my condition, and he put me on his shoulders, carrying me with as much ease as if I were only his knapsack. That night we camped in a swamp, without blankets ourselves; but Kistler soon captured one for me. A little raw meat was served next morning, and we were off, — I so sore, that only by bringing up the very utmost of my powers I travelled on.

That day at about two P. M. I could stand it no longer, for our road was up, up, always up the mountain. I threw myself down by the road, telling the.lieutenant they might leave me, parole me, or shoot me, I had no choice, but to walk one step further I would not. He told one of the guard to stay with me till a government wagon came up, and then bring me on to the Warm Springs, where he would camp till next day. So all marched on. My guard was an ignorant Tennesseean; and after talking to me a little, I pretended to sleep. He was lying near me, a little off from the road, in the woods. I soon noticed him sleeping, even snoring. I took his gun in my hand and thought how easy I might put an end to him. " Murder," responded my conscience, " to kill a sleeping, ignorant man." I knew that for me to go away would be folly: I could not walk the fourth of a mile. In an hour, the wagons came up, and I was put in with three wounded Rebels. At dark we came to the Warm Springs, and found our boys in camp by the side of a brick church. Flour had been given them, but nothing to cook it with. So we mixed it up with water into thick paste, wrapped it on sticks, and held it over the embers till cooked.

Next morning, we were paraded by the drunken lieutenant before the large hotel, for the criticism of the guests. After going through this disagreeable inspection, we were marched over the Warm Spring Mountain, to Bath Alum Springs, where we were once more paraded, for the amusement of the fashionable first families. Resuming our march, we came to within five miles of Millsborough Station, which was our destination; but as it was climbing mountains all the time, I gave out, once more refusing to walk; so a guard was left with me, with orders, after I rested, to walk slowly on, and if we got to Millsborough after the train had gone, to put me in the jail and leave me. This was sad, for I wanted to go on with Captain Bense, Lieutenant Shafer, Lieutenant Gilman, and Kistler, with whom I had formed such pleasant acquaintance, and from whom I had received so much kindness. While we sat by the way, a spring-wagon drove by, with two Rebel officers sitting on the front seat. We asked to ride. They said they were taking the remains of Colonel Washington to Millsborough, and could not make time for the train if they took us in.

As they passed by, a negro, driving three galled and broken-down mules, came up.

" Where are you driving those mules, boy?"

" Gwine to pastor 'em at Millsborough, massa."

" I must ride one of them, then," said I.

" I got no 'jections, massa. Mighty 'fraid dat animal can't hold you up, though."

The guard put me on the bare-backed and bridleless mule, and walked behind, urging him up with his bayonet occasionally. We were soon up with our men, who all laughed and cheered as I passed by them. I heard Captain Bense say, " It's hard to tell who looks the worse for wear, the man or the mule."

At four P. M. we arrived at Millsborough, and in half an hour, sixteen of us were put into a box-car, in most uncomfortable quarters, and at ten P. M. we were in the city of Staunton, where we were marched to an old depot, into which straw had been put for our accommodation. I had no sooner touched the straw than I was sleeping soundly; but I was soon awakened by the noise of a drunken Rebel officer, who was swearing at a great rate, and waking up the prisoners, to ask them where they were from, and what they came down here for. This first-family man flourished a huge knife, and told how many men he could kill with it. At length he disturbed the wrong man, when he got hold of a red-haired sergeant of the Sixth Ohio Regiment, who drew himself up in Heenan style and told the F. F. V. in strong language, that, if he did not let him go to sleep, he would kill him. The F. F. V. did not use his knife, but swore vengeance next morning. But when we marched out at daylight, I suppose this Confederate officer was sleeping off his drunk; and we marched to the depot, and were off to Richmond, where we arrived at six P. M. of, I think, the third day of October. We were marched down Main Street amidst the hooting of soldiers and the shouts of ragged little boys. " D—d Yankee!" was all the sound we could hear. At the lower end of Main Street is situated several tobacco-factories. We were drawn up in line in front of the officers' quarters, which at that time was in Ligon & Co.,s factory. Here the roll was called, and a drunken lieutenant put down the names, rank, when and where captured, charges, &c.

My name was called last. I was just going to give my regiment, when the lieutenant who had come with us said, "That man was captured several months ago as a spy, and has been in jail at Huntersville."

I was heart-sick, for I thought I was free from that charge. We stood there in the street till it was quite dark, when we were marched into a factory opposite. The guards threw up their guns, and we walked in amid the noise and bustle of a soldier-prison. The rooms were very large, and the gas burning brightly. Here were men from every State, in all sorts of uniforms, laughing, singing, playing cards, and seeming very happy. We soon scattered through the building. Each new-comer was the centre of some questioning crowd. Before we had been in half an hour, I heard some two shots fired at the new prisoners who had foolishly gone near a third-story window. In this way they told us several had been killed within two weeks..

Next morning the sergeant came to call the roll, and ordered all new prisoners to stand on the east side of the room. He then commenced to call our names. But he found that his roll, written by the drunken lieutenant, was not readable, and he called up one of his sergeants to copy it for him on a blank, which he had with him. When he came to my name, Captain Bense, who read the names off, instead of reading my name as "captured in July as a spy," read, "captured in September, at Elk Water; belonging to the Sixth Regiment Indiana Volunteers." The sergeant now called the roll; then said, "All commissioned officers step two paces to the front." Captain Bense, Lieutenant Gilman, and Lieutenant Shafer went out. Bense looked back, seeing me, and said, "There is Dr. Fletcher, Assistant Surgeon of the Sixth Regiment." I took the hint, and was marched off with them to the officers' quarters.

We found some sixty Federal officers just at breakfast. Good bread, beefsteak, and coffee seemed to abound; and I for one did justice to these rarities; and the result was that in half an hour I was deadly sick. I found no one to talk to. All our officers shunned me, for I was lean, long-haired, ragged, and dirty. They were fat, slick, and in their new uniforms, which they had worn on the Bull-Run field.

But in time I became well acquainted with all the officers, received money from home, and spent as agreeable times as a prisoner could be expected to. I used every endeavor to learn if Clark was in Richmond; but he was not there. I heard that a man of that description had been sent to New Orleans.

# ROSTERS OF REGIMENTS.

## SIXTH INDIANA.

THREE MONTHS, FROM APRIL 25, 1861.

*Colonel:* THOMAS T. CRITTENDEN.
*Lieut.-Colonel:* HIRAM PRATHER.
*Major:* JOHN GERBER.
*Quartermaster:* JOSIAH H. ANDREWS.
*Surgeons:* CHARLES SCHUESSLER; JOHN W. DAVIS.

| *Captains.* | *First Lieutenants.* | *Second Lieutenants.* |
|---|---|---|
| T. T. Crittenden, *A.* | P. P. Baldwin, *A.* | S. Russell, *A.* |
| Philem. P. Baldwin, *A.* | Samuel Russell, *A.* | Isaac Stephens, *A.* |
| Augustus H. Abbett, *B.* | Allen W. Prather, *B.* | William C. Wheeler, *B.* |
| Charles Childs, *C.* | Rich. W. Meredith, *C.* | Alanson Solomon, *C.* |
| Thom. J. Harrison, *D.* | Thomas Herring, *D.* | William R. Phillips, *D.* |
| Jerem. C. Sullivan, *E.* | John Gerber, *E.* | R. W. Gale, *E.* |
| John Gerber, *E.* | R. W. Gale, *E.* | J. T. Hendricks, *E.* |
| Rufus W. Gale, *E.* | John T. Hendricks, *E.* | William Hamilton, *E.* |
| Will. C. Moreau, *F.* | Robert Allison, *F.* | John Cole, *F.* |
| Hagaman Tripp, *G.* | Josiah H. Andrews, *G.* | George W. Kendrick, *G.* |
| Fielder A. Jones, *H.* | Stephen Story, *H.* | Calvin B. Trumbo, *H.* |
| John D. Evans, *I.* | John F. Longley, *I.* | George A. Wainwright, *I.* |
| Alois O. Bachman, *K.* | George W. Wiley, *K.* | William T. Days, *K.* |

## SEVENTH INDIANA.

### THREE MONTHS, FROM APRIL 25, 1861.

*Colonel:* EBENEZER DUMONT.
*Lieut.-Colonel:* BENJAMIN J. SPOONER.
*Major:* SAMUEL P. OYLER.
*Adjutant:* JAMES GAVIN.
*Quartermaster:* DAVID E. SPARKS.
*Surgeons:* GEORGE W. NEW; WILLIAM GILLESPIE.

| *Captains.* | *First Lieutenants.* | *Second Lieutenants.* |
|---|---|---|
| James Burgess, *A.* | Peter S. Kennedy, *A.* | Joseph S. Miller, *A.* |
| James Morgan, *B.* | Ira G. Grover, *B.* | Benjamin Ricketts, *B.* |
| John M. Blair, *C.* | John Flynn, *C.* | John C. Maze, *C.* |
| B. J. Spooner, *D.* | D. E. Sparks, *D.* | Jesse Armstrong, *D.* |
| John F. Cheek, *D.* | Jesse Armstrong, *D.* | Eli Matlock, *D.* |
| John H. Ferry, *E.* | Henry Waller, *E.* | Alexander B. Pattison, *E.* |
| J. V. Bemusdaffer, *F.* | James Gavin, *F.* | B. C. Shaw, *F.* |
| Nathan Lord, Jr., *G.* | Benjamin C. Shaw, *F.* | Josephus L. Tucker, *F.* |
| S. P. Oyler, *H.* | L. K. Stevens, *G.* | William Francis, *G.* |
| Joseph P. Gill, *H.* | William B. Ellis, *H.* | W. B. McLaughlin, *H.* |
| John W. Rabb, *I.* | Solomon Waterman, *I.* | David Lostutter, *I.* |
| Jefferson K. Scott, *K.* | Charles Day, *K.* | Theodore Orner, *K.* |

## EIGHTH INDIANA.

### THREE MONTHS, FROM APRIL 25, 1861.

*Colonel:* WILLIAM P. BENTON.
*Lieut.-Colonel:* SILAS COLGROVE.
*Major:* DAVID SHUNK.
*Adjutants:* A. IRWIN HARRISON; CHARLES O. HOWARD.
*Quartermaster:* JOHN T. ROBINSON.
*Surgeons:* JAMES FORD; GEORGE W. EDGERLE.

| Captains. | First Lieutenants. | Second Lieutenants. |
|---|---|---|
| Jacob Widaman, *A.* | Francis C. Swiggett, *A.* | George Adams, *A.* |
| D. Shunk, *B.* | O. H. P. Carey, *B.* | John Reuss, *B.* |
| Oliver H. P. Carey, *B.* | John Reuss, *B.* | Jacob M. Wells, *B.* |
| S. Colgrove, *C.* | E. M. Ives, *C.* | Allen O. Neff, *C.* |
| Thomas J. Lee, *C.* | G. W. Edgerle, *D.* | William Fisher, *D.* |
| Thomas J. Brady, *D.* | Joseph Kirk, *D.* | Nathan Branson, *D.* |
| H. T. Vandevender, *E.* | John T. Robinson, *E.* | James Fergus, *E.* |
| Frederick Tykle, *F.* | James Fergus, *E.* | L. D. M'Callister, *E.* |
| Reuben A. Riley, *G.* | Henry Ray, *F.* | Joseph W. Connel, *F.* |
| O. O. Howard, *H.* | Henry C. Rariden, *G.* | George W. H. Riley, *G.* |
| Alex. J. Kenney, *H.* | William R. Walls, *G.* | Robert A. Douglass, *H.* |
| W. P. Benton, *I.* | A. J. Kenney, *H.* | Isaac Thomas, *I.* |
| Maberry M. Lacy, *I.* | M. M. Lacy, *I.* | James Conner, *I.* |
| Charles S. Parrish, *K.* | A. I. Harrison, *I.* | Franklin Daily, *K.* |
| | Isaac Thomas, *I.* | |
| | Jos. M. Thompson, *K.* | |

## NINTH INDIANA.

**THREE MONTHS, FROM APRIL 25, 1861.**

*Colonel:* ROBERT H. MILROY.
*Lieut.-Colonel:* DAVID M. DUNN.
*Major:* DON J. WOODWARD.
*Adjutant:* HENRY LORING.
*Quartermaster:* CARTER L. VIGUS.
*Surgeons:* DANIEL MEEKER; MASON G. SHERMAN.

| *Captains.* | *First Lieutenants.* | *Second Lieutenants.* |
|---|---|---|
| Jehu C. Hannum, *A.* | John H. Gould, *A.* | W. A. Pigman, *A.* |
| William H. Blake, *B.* | Asahel K. Bush, *B.* | Alison Bailey, *B.* |
| Theodore F. Mann, *C.* | C. H. Kirkendall, *C.* | James D. Braden, *C.* |
| Thomas G. Dunn, *D.* | Clinton Weimer, *D.* | C. L. Vigus, *D.* |
| William P. Segur, *E.* | Henry A. Whitman, *E.* | Orlando W. Miles, *D.* |
| D. J. Woodward, *F.* | T. J. Patton, *F.* | William S. Story, *E.* |
| Thomas J. Patton, *F.* | George W. Carter, *F.* | G. W. Carter, *F.* |
| R. H. Milroy, *G.* | G. C. Moody, *G.* | Joseph Richards, *F.* |
| Gideon C. Moody, *G.* | Edw. P. Hammond, *G.* | E. P. Hammond, *G.* |
| Robert A. Cameron, *H.* | Isaac C. B. Suman, *H.* | Albert J. Guthridge, *G.* |
| Andrew Anderson, *I.* | Henry Loring, *I.* | G. A. Pierce, *H.* |
| Dudley H. Chase, *K.* | Henry J. Blowney, *I.* | H. J. Blowney, *I.* |
| | Frank P. Morrison, *K.* | Alexander Hamilton, *K.* |

## TENTH INDIANA.

**THREE MONTHS, FROM APRIL 25, 1861.**

*Colonels:* JOSEPH J. REYNOLDS; MAHLON D. MANSON.
*Lieut.-Colonel:* JAMES R. M. BRYANT.
*Majors:* M. D. MANSON; WILLIAM C. WILSON.
*Adjutants:* JOSEPH C. SUIT; REUBEN C. KISE.
*Quartermaster:* ZEBULON M. P. HAND.
*Surgeons:* THOMAS P. MCCREA; WILLIAM H. MYERS.

| Captains. | First Lieutenants. | Second Lieutenants. |
|---|---|---|
| Chris Miller, *A*. | John E. Naylor, *A*. | Alvin Gay, *A*. |
| J. R. M. Bryant, *B*. | D. Fleming, *B*. | L. T. Miller, *B*. |
| Dickson Fleming, *B*. | Levin T. Miller, *B*. | John F. Compton, *B*. |
| John W. Blake, *C*. | J. C. Suit, *C*. | S. W. Shortle, *C*. |
| Abram O. Miller, *C*. | Samuel W. Shortle, *C*. | James W. Blake, *C*. |
| W. C. Wilson, *D*. | Alexander Hogeland, *D*. | John Brower, *D*. |
| S. McKee Wilson, *D*. | John A. Stein, *E*. | Henry C. Tinney, *E*. |
| William Taylor, *E*. | Demetrius Parsley, *F*. | Isaac W. Sanders, *F*. |
| Ezra Olds, *F*. | J. H. Watson, *G*. | J. H. Vanarsdall, *G*. |
| M. D. Manson, *G*. | James H. Vanarsdall, *G*. | Ebenezer H. Morgan, *G*. |
| James H. Watson, *G*. | E. R. Bladen, *H*. | David N. Steele, *H*. |
| William Conklin, *H*. | John W. Perkins, *I*. | R. C. Kise, *I*. |
| William C. Kise, *I*. | R. T. Fahnestock, *K*. | Z. M. P. Hand, *K*. |
| Charles C. Smith, *K*. | | Benjamin F. Beitzell, *K*. |
| William H. Morgan, *K*. | | |

## ELEVENTH INDIANA.

### THREE MONTHS, FROM APRIL 25, 1861.

*Colonel:* LEWIS WALLACE.
*Lieut.-Colonel:* GEORGE F. McGINNIS.
*Majors:* CHARLES O. WOOD; WILLIAM J. H. ROBINSON.
*Adjutant:* DANIEL MACAULEY.
*Quartermaster:* HENRY L. RYCE.
*Surgeons:* THOMAS W. FRY; JOHN C. THOMPSON.

| Captains. | First Lieutenants. | Second Lieutenants. |
|---|---|---|
| Robert S. Foster, *A.* | George Butler, *A.* | J. H. Livsey, *A.* |
| George Butler, *A.* | Joseph H. Livsey, *A.* | David B. Hay, *A.* |
| John Fahnestock, *B.* | Orin S. Fahnestock, *B.* | D. B. Culley, *B.* |
| Charles W. Lyman, *B.* | Daniel B. Culley, *B.* | James F. Troth, *B.* |
| C. O. Wood, *C.* | John E. Moore, *C.* | Francis G. Scott, *C.* |
| Jesse E. Hamill, *C.* | Neville L. Brown, *D.* | Thomas F. Wells, *D.* |
| Jabez Smith, *D.* | Dan. Macauley, *E.* | Henry Tindall, *E.* |
| DeWitt C. Rugg, *E.* | Henry Tindall, *E.* | Nicholas R. Ruckle, *E.* |
| Edward T. Wallace, *F.* | John Stevenson, *F.* | Isaac M. Rumsey, *F.* |
| Henry M. Carr, *G.* | Harvey B. Wilson, *G.* | John W. Ramsay, *F.* |
| W. J. H. Robinson, *H.* | F. Knefler, *H.* | John F. Caven, *G.* |
| Frederick Knefler, *H.* | Thom. W. Fry, Jr., *H.* | Wallace Foster, *H.* |
| Lew. Wallace, *I.* | Abram C. Wilson, *I.* | I. C. Elston, Jr., *I.* |
| Isaac C. Elston, Jr., *I.* | Wm. W. Darnall, *K.* | John W. Ross, *I.* |
| G. F. McGinnis, *K.* | J. A. McLaughlin, *K.* | William Dawson, *K.* |
| William W. Darnall, *K.* | | |

## TWELFTH INDIANA.

ONE YEAR, FROM MAY 15, 1861.

*Colonels:* JOHN M. WALLACE; WILLIAM H. LINK.
*Lieut.-Colonels:* W. H. LINK; GEORGE HUMPHREY.
*Majors:* G. HUMPHREY; HENRY HUBLER.
*Adjutants:* JOHN W. MOORE; OSCAR N. HINKLE; CYRUS J. MCCOLE.
*Quartermaster:* MILTON R. DIXON.
*Surgeons:* WILLIAM H. LOMAX; ISAAC CASSELBERRY; JOHN H. COOK; NOBLE P. HOWARD.
*Chaplain:* JOSIAH P. WATSON.

| Captains. | First Lieutenants. | Second Lieutenants. |
|---|---|---|
| Thomas G. Morrison, *A.* | J. W. Moore, *A.* | J. A. M. Cox, *A.* |
| Thomas R. Noel, *B.* | John A. M. Cox, *A.* | David M. Jordan, *A.* |
| James Bachman, *C.* | Sol. D. Kempton, *B.* | Daniel Stockwell, *B.* |
| William O'Brien, *D.* | Michael Kirchner, *C.* | James Huston, *B.* |
| H. Hubler, *E.* | C. J. McCole, *D.* | James W. Wallace, *C.* |
| Reuben Williams, *E.* | Patrick A. Gallagher, *E.* | George W. Collins, *C.* |
| G. Humphrey, *F.* | H. B. DuBarry, *F.* | John T. Floyd, *D.* |
| George Nelson, *F.* | O. N. Hinkle, *F.* | R. Williams, *E.* |
| W. H. Link, *G.* | William W. Angell, *G.* | Andrew S. Millice, *E.* |
| Arthur F. Reed, *G.* | George W. Steele, *H.* | G. Nelson, *F.* |
| Thomas R. Doan, *H.* | A. Buchanan, *I.* | John M. Godown, *F.* |
| Howell D. Thompson, *I.* | William Wood, *I.* | A. F. Reed, *G.* |
| Alexander Buchanan, *I.* | Benjamin S. Ayers, *K.* | Elbert D. Baldwin, *G.* |
| Joseph F. Draper, *K.* | | William E. Wallace, *H.* |
| | | William Carroll, *H.* |
| | | William Wood, *I.* |
| | | Alfred B. Taylor, *I.* |
| | | John M. Dixon, *K.* |

## SIXTEENTH INDIANA.

ONE YEAR, FROM MAY 14, 1861.

Colonel: PLEASANT A. HACKLEMAN.
Lieut.-Colonel: THOMAS J. LUCAS.
Major: JOEL WOLFE.
Adjutant: ROBERT CONOVER.
Quartermasters: LEWIS BURK; HENRY B. HILL.
Surgeons: ELIAS FISHER; GEORGE F. CHITTENDEN.
Chaplain: EDWARD JONES.

| Captains. | First Lieutenants. | Second Lieutenants. |
|---|---|---|
| Th. A. McFarland, A. | David T. Sleeth, A. | Robert Conover, A. |
| John S. Lee, B. | Thomas Reading, B. | Wm. H. F. Randall, A. |
| James P. Gillespie, C. | Henry B. Austin, C. | John H. Finley, B. |
| John C. McQuiston, D. | William H. Weyer, D. | Charles P. Williamson, C. |
| Joseph Marshall, E. | William H. Greer, E. | Conrad Shomber, D. |
| John M. Orr, E. | P. J. Beachbard, F. | Thomas J. Powell, E. |
| Joel Wolfe, F. | Robert J. Price, F. | John M. Hartley, E. |
| Paul J. Beachbard, F. | John L. Groves, F. | R. J. Price, F. |
| T. J. Lucas, G. | A. G. Dennis, G. | Daniel Stricker, F. |
| Albert G. Dennis, G. | William J. Fitch, G. | Silas D. Byram, F. |
| William Judkins, H. | Henry L. Francis, H. | W. J. Fitch, G. |
| John A. Platter, I. | William Copeland, I. | Philip Dexheimer, G. |
| Alfred J. Hawn, K. | Robert E. Smith, K. | Samuel Tull, H. |
| | | Israel Phalin, I. |
| | | Courtland C. Matson, K. |

www.ingramcontent.com/pod-product-compliance
Lightning Source LLC
Chambersburg PA
CBHW030336170426
43202CB00010B/1139